This Moment Is Your Life

(AND SO IS  THIS ONE)

A Fun and Easy Guide to MINDFULNESS, MEDITATION, and YOGA

MARIAM GATES

Illustrated by LIBBY VANDERPLOEG

Dial Books

DIAL BOOKS

An imprint of Penguin Random House LLC

375 Hudson Street, New York, NY 10014

Text copyright © 2018 by Mariam Gates

Illustrations copyright © 2018 by Libby VanderPloeg

Printed in China • ISBN 9780399186622

1 3 5 7 9 10 8 6 4 2

Design by Jason Henry

Text set in Neutraface Slab Text

For Marah Bianca Rhoades
For everything

Contents

Introduction

Imagine you are walking into your school. See it all as clearly as you can: Notice what's on the walls, feel the weight of your backpack on your shoulders, hear the sound of the bell. Who do you see? What are you looking forward to? What is uncomfortable? How do you feel?

You are learning history, math, science, English, and maybe even how to speak another language. But you don't have a class on how to handle your thoughts and feelings. There aren't instructions for how to take care of yourself and manage your complicated life.

Even a normal day of school can be enough to make you feel completely overwhelmed.

Maybe you aren't playing well in a game, and you get a bad grade on a project because you misunderstood the directions, and a friend seems annoyed but you don't know why.

At your age, you have a lot more responsibilities than you

used to. Not that long ago, your parents made most of your plans and decisions, but now you are choosing how to spend your time and who to spend it with. You are in charge of how much energy you put into your grades, sports, theater, or whatever else is in your life. There is more to keep track of and more to worry about. Everything is competing for your attention, and that creates stress.

Stress can make you sad or angry. It can build up to the point where you want to scream or even hit something. You can feel stress in your body—as tension in your neck and shoulders, stomachaches and headaches, shortness of breath, or tiredness. Stress can make it hard to fall asleep at night, which then makes everything even worse. When you have a lot on your mind it is difficult to stop and get some perspective.

I procrastinate a lot with my homework and then I feel like I can't even start. Every day there are more things on my to-do list and not enough of them are getting checked off. My sister and I share a room, so when I'm trying to get things done I end up yelling at her over any sound she makes. When I'm overwhelmed I get headaches.

—Allison, age 12

Even when you aren't worrying about something specific, your mind can feel busy. Your mind can feel like a monkey swinging through the jungle from tree to tree. Just when you land, your thoughts take off in another direction. With this "monkey mind" you never really get to rest because there is always something new to focus on. It can feel as if your thoughts are just spiraling from thing to thing with no end.

Whether you're distracted by something you are worried about or just juggling a lot at once, the results are the same. When your thoughts are going a million miles a minute, you miss out on what is happening in the only time that exists—now.

It makes sense to want to get to the next moment, the next experience. It is part of being human to always be looking for the next possibility. If you are alone, you are thinking about when you'll be with your friends; if it is Sunday you are focused on how Monday is going to go. You don't let yourself be in this moment because it always feels like the important experience, event, or thing is the one coming up next.

But this is a problem. Because your life is only ever happening right here, right now.

This is the moment that exists. This is the only place you will ever be able to enjoy or experience anything.

The good news is that you can teach your mind to be in this

moment happily and with ease. Learning how to be here now is the best way to manage everything that goes on in your life. If you are present, you can handle it.

What you will find is that 90 percent of the time, this moment, the one you are in right now, is just fine (and also very manageable). There may be things in the past or future that you are concerned about, but right here, right now, is okay.

Being completely present, even for a little while, can go a long way. It can help you feel more comfortable, confident, and even happy dealing with everything you experience on a regular basis.

Unplugging from Your Thoughts and Plugging into the Present

Sit up tall, and let your body relax.
Take a deep breath in, then let a long breath out.
Notice the calm here in the present.
This moment is just fine.

None of this is new information. All of the tools and techniques in this book have been used for thousands of years. People realized a long time ago that our constant rush of thoughts often makes us distracted and unhappy. We imagine worrisome outcomes for the future and we rehash unfortunate things that have already occurred. As a result, the life that is happening in this moment gets ignored. People discovered that the more we pay attention to what is happening right now, the more rational and relaxed we become.

Today, mindfulness practices are used by successful people in every field: CEOs of Fortune 500 companies, Silicon Valley innovators, teachers, professional athletes, and Oscar-winning actors and producers. There is plenty of information available about how these techniques can support you. But don't take this book's word for it. Experience it for yourself!

In each chapter you will find simple techniques for using mindfulness (awareness of your internal and external environment) to let go of stress and be present. It is up to you to find out if they are helpful. It is up to you to see if they make things easier.

This book is about creating new habits. Everything you'll find here is called a "practice" (a mindfulness practice, a yoga practice, etc.) because each one is something you'll need to practice before it will work well for you. Each of these techniques will

The tree that
BENDS
doesn't
BREAK

help you build your own internal resiliency. Each one will help you get better at coping with stress and making good choices, no matter "which way the wind is blowing" through your life.

You want to be "the tree that bends"—able to feel rooted and strong but relaxed and flexible in the midst of whatever is happening around you. The key to happiness is being able to be comfortable in this moment, here and now.

How to Use This Book

For the purpose of this book we are going to look at mindfulness, yoga, breathing, and meditation as separate chapters, but of course they overlap. If you are focusing while in a yoga pose, you are using mindfulness (an awareness of your senses), and if you are in seated meditation, you may be paying attention to your breath, etc. It is helpful to look at each practice individually to learn about them, but all of these techniques and tools are pointing you toward the same result: being fully present for whatever is happening in this moment.

Each chapter will focus on specific elements of these ancient practices. The yoga chapter, for example, will outline how to use the physical practice of asana, and the meditation chapter will discuss the seated technique of being aware of thought patterns. There is far more to study and understand about each of the chapters' practices as well as many other approaches. The resources listed at the end of the book provide more information.

You can read this book straight through and then come

back to the exercises that are most interesting to you. Or, you can just turn to any of the chapters and begin there. Each section is designed to give you practical ways to bring all of the benefits of mindfulness into your life. And in the final chapter you'll find five-day challenges that map out for you ways to pull all of the book's mindfulness techniques together in your everyday life.

Throughout each chapter there are **Try It** exercises that give you a way to immediately feel what is being described. There may be concepts in the book that are new to you, but once you do a "Try It," you will have a firsthand experience. Reading about these techniques is a good place to start, but nothing is better than actually testing how they work for you.

At the end of each chapter is a **Tool Kit** of helpful exercises. You can go through all of the techniques in the tool kit or pick a few and see how they feel.

Most importantly, have fun with everything you find here. Mindfulness practices sound very quiet and serious, but their purpose is to help you feel relaxed and comfortable and to enjoy the moment!

Life becomes more meaningful WHEN YOU REALIZE THE SIMPLE FACT THAT YOU'LL NEVER GET THE SAME MOMENT TWICE.

Right now. Before you read any further.

Feel all the points where your body is making contact with your chair or your bed (wherever you are reading right now).

Notice the temperature of the air as you take your next breath in and then let it out.

Get still for a moment and start to pay attention to the sounds of the people or anything around you in the room.

Notice how you feel in your body. Is any part of your body tense? Relaxed?

Now take a deep breath in and let a long breath out.

This simple awareness of yourself in the room is enough to shift your mind from a state of distraction to clarity in the moment.

The idea is not to stop thinking—you can't!—but to be able to pause and notice where you are and how you are feeling. Paying attention to what it is like to sit here right now is a good place to begin.

CHAPTER ONE

Mindfulness

Mindfulness is paying attention to this moment on purpose. It is simply asking the question "What is happening right now?" It is noticing your thoughts, feelings, and the environment without judging any of it as good or bad. It is simply being present with curiosity.

There's a story about two monks walking from one village to another. They come upon a woman who can't get past a muddy section of the road. The older monk puts the woman on his back and carries her over the mud. The whole time she is berating him for being too slow and for splashing her. When they get to the other side, he puts her down, and the two monks walk on.

An hour later the older monk asks the younger one why he looks upset.

"That woman was so rude to you," he answers.

"My friend," says the older monk. "I put that woman down an hour ago. You are still carrying her."

As you are reading right now, your brain is processing the information on the page but also moving at light speed through thoughts, feelings, and reactions—some of which have to do with this book and some of which surely do not. It is normal to have a very active

mind, but it is important to know how to use it to see what is in front of you. It is easy to be like that second monk: distracted by the past instead of present in the current moment.

The Stress Reaction

It is not surprising that there is a lot going on inside your head. Your brain is the control center for everything. It keeps your heart beating, and it is how you can choreograph a dance, learn Spanish, and cry during a sad movie.

When you get upset, panicked, or angry, your whole body goes into a reaction known as the "fight or flight" response. Your blood pressure rises, your pupils dilate, and your heart rate and breathing speed up. Under stress, the most primitive part of your brain, the brain stem, sends messages to your body to prepare to defend (fight) or retreat to safety (flight).

People call that part of the brain the "lizard brain" because its functions are those of basic survival that humans and reptiles share. This area of the brain does not do any of your complex thinking and only cares about one thing: attacking or fleeing when it perceives danger.

This reactive part of your brain does its job well, but it cannot distinguish between real danger and more general worries. Whether you are escaping from a tiger or fretting about a book report that's due tomorrow, the body responds in a similar way. Even a small amount of stress (something as simple as forgetting something at home, or a moment of feeling awkward or left out) can switch your whole system into survival mode. You can easily respond from your lizard brain whether you're dealing with big or small challenges.

Maybe you've already noticed a shift in your own body when you realize there's a quiz today or you're angry about something someone said. Do your arms tense, your palms clench, or does your face feel hot? Maybe there's a noticeable change in your breathing and heart rate as your body prepares to protect you. That is your "lizard brain" taking control of the situation.

*I feel overwhelmed by how much I have to do sometimes.
I get worried that I didn't understand an assignment or
I'm going to forget something important, and it makes
me feel pain in my shoulders and neck. I also get
stomachaches a lot.* —Rebecca, age 14

*There are kids at school who pick on the younger kids.
Sometimes even my friends do that and I don't want
to be a part of it but I also don't feel like I can tell them to
stop. When that happens it's hard to catch my breath, my jaw
feels really tight, and my whole body feels overworked
and exhausted.* —Mateo, age 13

These reactions are your brain and body working to keep you safe when sensing a threat, and overall that is a good thing. But studies show that sustained time spent in the fight or flight mode is dangerous for your health. Usually your immune cells function like Pac-Man, searching out disease cells and chomping them before they can multiply. Under stress, the body releases hormones like cortisol, which cause the entire immune system to slow down dramatically so that most of your energy can be channeled to the threat at hand. However, when those immune cells slow down, more disease cells stick around, weakening your system.

The Mindfulness Response

Mindfulness deactivates that stress reaction. It is like giving your whole system a Pac-Man Power Pellet. Using the brain to pay attention to the present has been shown to reduce stress in the mind and body and actually improve your ability to manage challenges. When you can be present and aware of how you are feeling in this moment, your body stops releasing excess hormones and returns to a more balanced state. This response is called "rest and renew," and it is when your body returns to its natural state of well-being. When we are calm and clearheaded, the parts of our brain that are in charge of emotions (the "mammalian" brain) and thinking (the "human" brain) can function and bring perspective to what is actually going on. (Is there a tiger or are we simply doing challenging homework?)

Bottom line: Mindfulness is a simple way to de-stress and actually improve brain functioning. Students who practice mindfulness show less anxiety in social and academic situations and report a higher sense of accomplishment and well-being.

The shift from fight or flight to rest and renew is always available. Just one deep breath in and one long breath out can change how you feel mentally and physically.

Pausing even for a moment has a profound effect on your ability to respond to your situation. If there is a real issue you need to address, being present will give you the clarity to make the best choice for yourself and others.

Listening Exercise

For the next thirty seconds you are going to be still and focus on your sense of hearing. (Set a timer if you have one. Otherwise, just estimate. You may want to read through the exercise first.)

Sit comfortably. Place your hands in your lap or on your knees. Close your eyes or look down so that you are less distracted by what you see and can focus on what you hear.

Begin: Pay attention to everything you hear outside of the room: cars, the wind, birds, people. What do you hear that you usually don't even notice?

Now what do you hear inside the room? Any small noises you couldn't hear until you were quiet?

Can you hear anything in your own body? Your breathing? Your heartbeat?

Take a deep breath in and let a long breath out. What do you notice?

How do you feel?

Getting quiet and listening is a simple way of pausing to notice where you are. Even in that short time period, your breathing most likely became slower, and your brain and body received the message that there was no need to rev up. There are a lot of benefits to being able to pause, even for thirty seconds, to tune into the moment.

HABITS of the MIND

Clearly, the human brain has developed beyond the basic survival skills needed to escape mortal danger. But the way your brain processes information still has a few pitfalls. You can think of these as habits of the mind. Just as your "lizard brain" triggers automatic physical responses, these habits of the mind trigger automatic mental and emotional responses. The brain is just doing its job, but if you don't bring awareness and some alternative strategies to what is actually happening here and now, then these habits, these limited ways of using information, will end up running the show.

Let's look at three habits of the mind:

Negative Mind

(that with mindfulness can become Flexible Mind)

Stuck Mind

(that with mindfulness can become Open Mind)

Distracted Mind

(that with mindfulness can become Focused Mind)

Each of these habits can get in the way of seeing situations in your life clearly. We will look at them in detail because it will be helpful to see if you relate to any of them. But an easy way to understand whether you are stuck in a habit of the mind instead of being truly present is to take a quick inventory of how you feel. Do you feel more constricted and contracted like a closed fist? Or do you feel comfortable and accepting of what is, like an open palm? (This doesn't necessarily mean that you will always like what you are seeing or feeling. More on that later. What you'll be working on right now is the ability to be awake and clear about what is happening in the moment.)

DO YOU FEEL...

TIGHT in your BODY? (NECK, JAW, SHOULDERS, ARMS)

IS YOUR BREATHING CONSTRICTED? OR DO YOU FEEL RELAXED? IS YOUR BREATHING slow and easy?

WEST MIDDLE BASKETB

Mindfulness (being present and aware of how you are feeling and what you are sensing in the moment) is all that is needed to create a shift away from the unhealthy habits described here. See if any of these feel familiar to you as you read.

Negative Mind

Picture the way a bird is constantly scanning the area for danger, moving its head this way and that. A bird's survival depends on it staying alert. It does not help the bird to be still and notice what it is feeling. The bird needs to keep its attention on what might be dangerous in any situation. Over the course of our evolution, humans have also had to continuously scan for threats. We've learned to focus on the negative.

In most situations, however, things aren't all bad or all good. Drifting apart from a friend, for example, can feel sad and unsettling, but it does make space for new people and maybe new activities in your life. The loss of a friendship is not easy, but it is also not all bad.

Your mind is not wired for this kind of subtlety, and that can make you confused about what you are seeing. Like the bird, you want to get answers quickly to keep yourself safe. As humans we have trained ourselves to notice problems before anything positive in a situation. But this thinking can become very limited very quickly.

If you see a field of flowers with a snake in it, you focus on the snake.

Noticing a snake is important, and again, that instinct is a part of your biology

that keeps you safe. That is where your "lizard brain" is working for you. If there is a viper in front of you, you want your mind to react quickly. However, your habit of scanning for threats can cause you to miss out on the flowers (or anything else pleasant) that is right in front of you.

You can see that same survival instinct being triggered in a room full of people. Have you ever been in a group situation in which one person makes a comment you don't like or doesn't listen to you, and then that one thing is what you focus on for the rest of the time? You can easily ignore everything that was positive about the situation, and spend all of your time thinking about the one thing that was not. This is negative mind. In the wild, that focus on danger is helpful, but in your day-to-day life, not so much.

There's a very old story about a farmer and his family in a small village. One day, the farmer's son finds a wild stallion and brings it home. He is overjoyed to show his father.

"Look what great fortune! Now I have this incredible horse!" His father replies, "Good luck, bad luck, who knows?"

A week later, the boy is out riding and falls and breaks his leg. He is angry and distraught, and tells his father how upset he is that such a horrible thing has happened to him.

His father's response is again: "Good luck, bad luck, who knows?" A week after that, the army of the king arrives and demands that all young men join them in a new and terrible war. The farmer's son with his broken leg cannot go.

Again, the farmer's response is the same: "Good luck, bad luck, who knows?"

It is a story about perspective. We all have reactions to what happens in our lives, and those reactions are not wrong. But without perspective, we tend to see things in only one way. Mindfulness creates an opportunity to recognize the negative mind. When you are present for what is really happening right here, right now, you are less likely to jump to conclusions (and make assumptions) about people, situations, and what you think you know. You can appreciate what is positive. You can understand and have compassion for your habit of looking for threats and see that almost everything has multiple layers and is usually not all good or all bad.

*You know you are in **Negative Mind** when:*

• you have no perspective (you are focused—sometimes almost
obsessively—on what is or might not be good in a situation)

• you feel you need to get your own way

• your body is tense (tight chest, jaw, arms, or fists,
strain in your neck and shoulders, shortened breath)

 *You know you are in **Flexible Mind** when:*

• you understand that you might not know
all the sides of a situation

• you trust that things will work out even if you are
not sure exactly how

• your body is relaxed (no strain in your shoulders, neck, and
arms, your breathing is slow and easy, your chest feels open)

WE CAN COMPLAIN BECAUSE
THE ROSEBUSHES HAVE
thorns,
OR REJOICE BECAUSE
THE THORN BUSHES HAVE
roses

— ABRAHAM LINCOLN —

 **Stuck Mind**

The mind often uses past experiences to assess new situations. This kind of learning shortcut works well in some cases. A baby learns that the oven is not safe because she can feel that it is hot. If she goes to someone else's house, she won't touch that stove either. She is learning new information.

In other situations, your mind's tendency to rely on what you felt or saw in the past can keep you stuck. If you tried something and it was hard, you don't want to try it again. If something scared you in the past, you avoid it without question. You are in a stuck habit of the mind when you have a rigid belief about what should or shouldn't happen. If you are not paying attention in the present moment, there is no room for new data. You'll end up using experiences from the past to dictate your future. You can't grow. You can't stretch. You can't change.

Menu

FAVORITES
- No Risk and No Possibility of Failure
- Whatever We Did/ Thought 3 Years Ago
- Things We're Sure We Can Do

CHEF'S SPECIAL
- Information from the Past (with a Side of Fries)

DISCONTINUED
- Trying New Things
- Learning What We're Capable of
- Being Vulnerable
- Risking Failure
- Being Courageous

If you aren't clear about what you feel and who you are now, you end up making decisions for yourself as a teenager based on how something was for you when you were only seven.

I was in a dance performance in second grade and I wasn't as good as the other kids, so no, I'm not going to try this new modern dance class at school.

Or you make decisions because of what you are afraid of rather than what is happening here and now.

I've never skied and most of my friends have. I don't want to look foolish, so I'm not going to go on that ski trip.

Or you let what you think should be happening get in the way of dealing with what is happening.

I'm not going to ask that teacher for extra help. My brother did well in this class. I don't want anyone to know I don't understand.

Today, right now, is a new moment you have never experienced before. If you can't pause and see that, you really limit your options. This moment is happening for the first time. It is full of potential. If you are caught in beliefs about the past and your fears, you end up being a reactor instead of an actor in your own life.

Is there something you haven't tried because you're not sure you'll succeed or be as good at it as someone else you know?

If your answer is yes, you are not alone. Remember, your mind wants to keep you protected. It wants to stay with what is familiar and use only past information for making decisions. But it's important to know the difference between being realistically cautious and letting old information wrongly dictate what you do now. When you are aware in the present moment, you can notice when that stuck mind is operating. That is where mindfulness comes in.

In this moment you can notice what you feel and ask yourself, *Am I using good judgment or an old, inhibiting way of seeing something? Do I feel stressed and fearful or relaxed and receptive?* If you can pause and feel present, you have a chance to open your mind to new approaches and ideas.

*You know you are in **Stuck Mind** when:*

- you feel misunderstood and grouchy

- you feel afraid of trying something new

- your body is tense and achy

*You know you are in **Open Mind** when:*

- you feel excited and curious about what you're doing

- you are willing to try new things

- your body is light and energized

May
your choices
reflect your
H🙂PES,
not your
FEARS

— NELSON MANDELA —

# Distracted Mind

Maybe you don't focus on the negative and you aren't stuck in old ideas about yourself. But you still have a busy human mind that makes it difficult to pay attention to the moment you are in right now.

Do you ever:

• Arrive someplace without really being aware of how you got there (maybe on your walk to school or moving from one class to another)?

• Go to get something in your room and forget what you needed once you are there?

• Check your phone for no particular reason even though you looked at it two minutes ago?

• Review the details of something that upset you over and over in your mind?

Again, welcome to having a brain. None of this is unique to you. We all share these habits in one form or another. It may seem like there are more distractions today (social media, phones, and socializing in an ever-increasing number of ways), but the issue of having a mind that won't "sit still" is in no way new. The techniques in this book were developed and used thousands of years ago because people were having the same problematic "monkey minds" then too. As a species we are good at using our brain to track hundreds of pieces of information at a time, but we're not so great at using it to focus on the here and now.

Even when you look relaxed, your mind can be traveling at warp speed. You're afraid of missing out, you review past conversations over and over in your mind, or you think about how much you have to do. Ring any bells? Without realizing it, you can easily lose track of where you are and what is happening now. Even imagining something good that you would like to have happen can take over your thoughts. It feels as if there is somewhere other than here that needs your attention—at all times.

We all live in a world of do-ing, not a world of be-ing. Being present may not even appear all that valuable.

It's tricky because this habit of staying out of the present moment does have benefits. You get complimented for being a productive multitasker. And reviewing your planner is important. Imagining scenarios for next weekend feels like a good use of your time. All of your many to-do lists do serve a purpose and keep you on track. There is a place for planning, but it seems to have taken over all of our lives, and you may find it difficult to operate in any other mode.

As a result, you can spend a lot more time in the past and the future than in the present.

Try It:

Take a Thinking Habits Self-Assessment

How often are your thoughts focused on something that happened in the past or that might happen in the future?

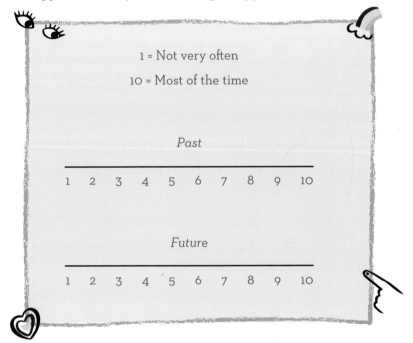

1 = Not very often

10 = Most of the time

Past

1 2 3 4 5 6 7 8 9 10

Future

1 2 3 4 5 6 7 8 9 10

Studies show that most stress comes from rehashing events that have already happened or from creating a story in the mind about things that might. You may find that your thinking tends to go more in one direction or the other. Either way, it is hard to be here and experience now when your thoughts are somewhere else.

*You know you are in **Distracted Mind** when:*

- you feel anxious and/or stressed

- you feel confused and/or your thoughts are racing

- your body feels achy and tight, and your
breathing is shallow

 *You know you are in **Focused Mind** when:*

- you are relaxed

- you are able to focus on one task at a time
(and it feels like enough)

- your body feels relaxed, energized, and you
are taking full breaths from your belly

Everyone has these habits of the mind to some degree. But it is possible to go from mind-full to mindful—from instinctual reacting to objective responding in the moment.

Life is happening right now, in real time, and that makes being in this moment very important. It takes skill to focus on the present and even more skill to feel relaxed and comfortable here. Being here now is how you address feeling negative, stuck, and busy. When you are present in the moment, those habits shift. You are more flexible, open, and focused. You can experience for yourself that in this exact moment, right here and now, there is rarely a problem.

Remember, mindfulness is something that has to be exercised like a muscle. When you are learning something new, it takes time to become skilled at it.

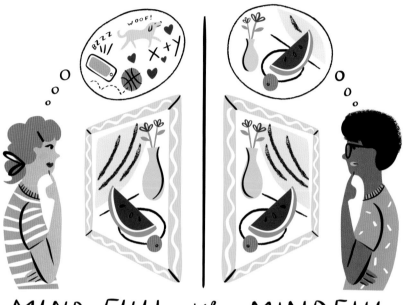

MIND-FULL vs. MINDFUL

Mindfulness in Your Body: Relaxed & Awake

In every mindfulness exercise, you begin by feeling relaxed and awake in your body. A relaxed and awake body is still, sitting or standing upright but not rigid, with shoulders loose and heart open.

When your body is energized but at ease, you are more able to pay attention to your thoughts, feelings, and sensations.

Try It:

Use your physical senses to be aware of this moment right now.

Find your version of a relaxed and awake body: still, upright but not rigid, at ease and open.

Now bring your attention to your breathing. Take a deep breath in, and feel your body fill as you inhale. Exhale, and feel the air move out of your body completely. Notice the rise and fall of your abdomen and chest as you continue to take easy breaths in and out.

Keep following your senses. What do you hear if you get very quiet?

What are you sitting on? How does it feel?

Where are your feet resting right now?

Pay attention for a moment to your neck and shoulders. Notice whether you are holding any tension there. Bring your awareness to your arms, your upper back, your lower back. Where do you feel tight, and where do you feel loose? Breathe.

What else do you notice when you pay attention to right here, right now?

Focusing on your physical senses is an easy way to shift your attention to the present. If you are in a stressful conversation, for example, you can immediately feel more comfortable by bringing your attention to your breathing and scanning your body for any tension and reactions as you listen.

Awareness • Acceptance = Mindfulness

We are all used to being told to calm down, to not get angry, and even to not cry. It is very important to note that mindfulness does not separate your emotions into good ones and bad ones; there is just this moment. With mindfulness, you are training yourself to be awake in this moment without trying to change this moment. (It's worth repeating that: Mindfulness is being awake in this moment without trying to change this moment.) It doesn't mean never changing anything about the

world or never addressing areas in your life where you are not happy. But any change has to start with seeing clearly. The skill you are developing is to feel and be, without adding judgments and reactions to the situation.

Being reactive or distracted can be a way to avoid dealing with your more difficult emotions. It can feel uncomfortable and at times painful to focus on where you are now. Letting your brain pop like popcorn from one thought to another can feel better than sitting for even a moment with something hard.

The problem is that here is the only place where you can actually experience anything. With mindfulness you can feel strong emotions and notice them without trying to make them go away or shove them down. If you can bring your attention to what it is like to be here in this room, in this moment, with these feelings, you will be much better at handling them. And if what you need is to talk to someone or get help, you'll be clearer about that too.

It is easy to confuse being present with being more relaxed. Often, being in the moment makes you feel more at ease, so that can be part of a description of being mindful. But mindfulness is not a practice of being calm. It is being aware of what is and being honest about it.

Nothing about this moment has to change. In this moment, the time it takes for you to take a full breath in and let it out, you are okay exactly as you are.

Just One Breath

Right now, pay attention to the next breath you take as it goes in and out through your nose. Notice everything you can as you breathe in. Focus on the point where air enters your body. Is the air cool? Is it warm? Breathe in fully.

Exhale. Do you notice movement in your chest and ribs? Does your abdomen rise and fall?

Now for the next two breaths, breathe slowly and feel your complete inhale—let the breath fill your stomach all the way to the very top of your torso, and then feel your complete exhale.

Breathe in . . . Breathe out . . . 1

Breathe in . . . Breathe out . . . 2

Now just breathe normally. Notice how you feel.

This moment is okay exactly as it is.

When you take care of the PRESENT, the FUTURE takes care of itself.

—JEFF MAZIAREK—

So, being present is not loud or dramatic, but it does have a radical effect on your life. As we've seen, the constant stream of worry and distraction drains you mentally and physically, and impacts your ability to manage what is in front of you. It can even rob you of your ability to change and grow and see what you are capable of. With mindfulness you bring all of your intelligence, creativity, and skill to the moment you are in. Right now. You have awareness and acceptance of whatever you are experiencing. You have kindness and compassion for yourself and the fact that your mind operates just like everyone else's. Whatever you're feeling, countless people have felt that way too. Mindfulness is a practice for every emotion, every experience. You don't have to change yourself or how you feel; you're just bringing awareness to it. If you are here, where life is happening, you can handle anything.

Calm and awake.

Just noticing.

Paying attention to this moment with curiosity and acceptance of what is.

Here and Now.

THAT IS MINDFULNESS.

When I pause and focus on my breath and how I am feeling, I end up feeling better. My soccer team lost in the finals and I really felt like we should have won. In the car on the way home I didn't try to tune it out like I would have before. I paid attention to my breath and felt how my chest was almost burning. By the time we got home, it's not like I didn't care, but I was not furious anymore and I did not feel so hot in my chest. I could have dinner with my family rather than just going to my room. I texted my friend who was the goalie to tell him he still did a good job even though we lost.

—Leo, age 13

When I try to pay attention to where I am right now, I usually stop worrying about things as much. I feel more separate from my problems instead of feeling like they are on top of me. I can be freaking out about whether a friend of mine told someone who I like. But when I realize I am in my room with my feet on the rug, listening to music, it feels more obvious that my fear and worry is mainly in my head. That whole situation is not happening here, in my room. Then I feel like, well, I'll deal with that if I need to. It's all more okay.

—Sophia, age 14

MINDFULNESS TOOL KIT

This is a collection of tools and techniques for practicing mindfulness. Use all of these exercises or just pick and choose the ones that appeal to you right now. Remember, mindfulness is a skill and a habit that is not hard to develop, but it does take practice. These exercises can help you feel better about being right here right now—whatever you are experiencing. Go at your own pace, be open, and see what happens.

Create Your Own Mindful Space

Try creating a peaceful spot in your room that will serve as a reminder to pause in your day. Maybe it is the top of your dresser, or a part of a shelf. When you look at it, it is your cue to notice how you are feeling now, in the present moment.

To create it, choose:

1. an item that has meaning to you
2. an item that makes you feel calm
3. an item from nature (which could be from outside or a photo or drawing)

This spot is now your visual reminder that all you need to do is pause, take a breath, and be here now.

Water Exercise

The shower is a great time to practice being in the moment. Next time you take a shower, pay attention to the water's temperature and the feeling of the beads of water on your head and skin. Notice the sensations. Notice everything you can about the smell of your soap, the texture of your shampoo, the steamy air around you. Be totally present for the experience.

You can do this same exercise while brushing your teeth. Feel the scrub of the bristles across your teeth and gums. Focus on the strong taste of the toothpaste. Notice every aspect of brushing your teeth. It is great practice for being present. You can even try brushing with the opposite hand. Breaking your regular routine brings you into the present moment, instead of operating on autopilot.

Squeeze and Release

This exercise can be done while you are reading right now. Just take your time and follow the prompts to notice and release any tension in your body.

- Take a deep breath in and fill your body.
  Exhale completely.

- Squeeze your feet. Curl each toe and hold it tight.
  Take a deep breath in and let it all out. Relax.

- Now try squeezing your feet and toes while flexing
  your legs. Get as tight as you can. Squeeze. Take a deep
  breath in . . . and a long breath out—release.

- Squeeze your feet, tighten up through your legs and
  stomach, and bring your shoulders toward your ears.
  Deep breath in . . . and a long breath out—release.

- Now you are going to squeeze everything:
  feet, legs, stomach, shoulders, arms, fists.
  Even squeeze your face: scrunch your mouth, nose,
  and eyes. Make it tight, tight, tight—squeeze.

- Take a deep breath in . . . then let it all out with a big sigh.

- Shake it out. You are done.

How do you feel?

Color Your Word

Choose a word that expresses how you feel right now. On a piece of paper, write the word in big bubble or block letters. Now choose your favorite pens or pencils to color it in.

Take your time. Pay attention to the shape of the paper, the smooth, flat surface and pointy edges. Get so quiet you can hear the sound of the pen or pencil on the page. How does it feel to move your hand across the paper? What colors are you drawn to?

Pay attention to how it feels to fill in the letters deeply and how it feels to just add a light brush of color. Vary it. If you find yourself criticizing your work, just notice that and remind yourself that there is no right way to do this. Keep going.

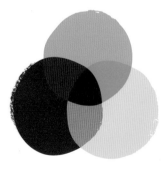

Eating Mindfully: The Chocolate Experience

Use this seeing, touching, smelling, hearing, and tasting exercise to be completely present . . . with chocolate!

1. Get a piece of chocolate. (If you can't eat chocolate, use a raisin.)

2. Take time to look at the colors and shapes on the packaging. (If the food is already out of the wrapper, skip to 5.)

3. Feel the weight of the chocolate in the palm of your hand.

4. Listen closely to the sound of the paper as you slowly unwrap the piece.

5. Hold the chocolate up to your nose and smell. What do you notice?

6. Before you eat the chocolate, notice if you have any feelings of impatience, distraction, excitement, or anything else.

7. Now take a bite (or put the whole piece in your mouth). Resist the urge to chew it, and notice everything you can about the texture, temperature, and taste. Is it all sweet, or is there some bitterness? What other flavors do you taste?

8. Savor it. Notice everything you can about how the chocolate feels in your mouth and on your tongue. Is it still in one piece? Is it starting to melt?

9. Enjoy the moment.

A Mindful Bite

You can bring the same awareness and focus from The Chocolate Experience to any meal. It is helpful to try having one mindful bite in each meal.

FOR JUST THAT ONE BITE, NOTICE:

- The color of the food
- The smell of the food

AS YOU SLOWLY TAKE THE MINDFUL BITE, NOTICE:

- The temperature of the food
- The consistency of the food
- Each of the different flavors (spicy, salty, sweet)
- How quickly or slowly you chew, and for how long

♪ Music on Your Mind

Choose a song or piece of music that you are familiar with, and see what it is like to focus on it completely. Play the music, and as you do, give it all of your attention. Listen as closely as you can and try to hear something you haven't noticed before.

- What instrument do you hear first?

- What other instruments do you hear? It doesn't matter if you know what they are called; just listen so closely that you hear something new.

- Do you hear more than one voice?

- Pay attention to where the music changes: where it gets faster, slower, louder, quieter.

- What do you feel when you listen to this music? Take a moment to focus only on your feelings.

Body Scan

Read all of these directions first, and then lie down to do the exercise. Keep the book next to you if you need to review. (After doing this exercise a couple of times, you won't need to refer to the book.)

You can lie down on your bed or on the floor. (It can be helpful to choose a harder surface like the floor, but do what is comfortable.)

• Close your eyes. Feel your breath as it comes in and out. Inhale. Exhale.

• Bring your awareness to your feet. Notice the bottoms of your feet, the tops of your feet, your toes.

• Now bring your awareness to your ankles. Shine your attention like a spotlight there, and feel any sensations.

• Bring your attention to your legs. Notice where the backs of your legs are touching the bed or the floor. Notice the sensations there as if you have never paid attention to your legs before.

• Feel your attention move to your hips.

• Let it move into your back, then your stomach, then your chest.

• Now shine that spotlight of attention onto your arms and all the way down to your hands. Be aware of each finger. Notice any sensations.

• Choose now to shift your attention to your shoulders. This is often a place of tension and stress. Just notice anything you can here. Don't try to change anything right now; just notice it.

• Now bring your awareness to your neck. The back of the neck, then the front, then the throat.

• Feel your attention move up to your face. Your jaw, your lips, your cheekbones, your nose, your eyes, around to your ears, back up to your forehead, and to the top of your head.

• Now bring your attention back to your breath. Inhale. Exhale.

• How do you feel?

Mindfulness at School

Door Handle Exercise:

Ahead of time, pick one class, one room where you are going to pause for a mindful moment. When you enter this room, notice your hand on the door. Does it have a knob, or is it a handle? Is it cold to the touch, does it move easily, or do you have to work it? This is your cue to pause and notice your surroundings and how you feel. Notice what you hear. If the door is already open, do the same practice when you sit down. Use your senses to notice your surroundings, feel your breath in and out, and be aware of how you are feeling. Whatever it is.

When you get home, reflect. Get out your journal and start writing:

In _____ class, I noticed _____.

One Breath:

Take a moment during your day to notice one breath in and one breath out. It does not need to be more complicated than that. Just check in, at some point—in math, at your locker, walking down the hall—to feel this moment. Notice one full breath in and one full breath out. See if you feel a little clearer, more focused, and better able to handle whatever is in front of you.

When you get home, reflect. Get out your journal and start writing.

I paused and focused on my breath
when I was _____.

I noticed _____.

Journaling

(You will need a journal for this next exercise)

• Go outside.

• Find a comfortable place to sit, and plan to stay in this spot for ten minutes.

• Look very closely at your surroundings. Write down everything you see, everything you feel, everything you hear, and everything you smell.

Write about the physical environment, the weather, and also your emotional state. Observe and put down everything that crosses your mind. If you want to, sketch what you see as well.

Take your time. Look very closely at your surroundings.

I see ——————————————— .

I smell ——————————————— .

I hear ——————————————— .

I touch ——————————————— .

I feel ——————————————— .

I am thinking about ——————————— .

I didn't expect ——————————— .

Mindfulness for Anger
and Other Difficult Emotions

We all have experiences that are unfair or infuriating, such as arguments with family or friends. When you are feeling angry, the idea behind mindfulness is not to stop being angry but instead to be comfortable with how it feels (even if it's intense).

The next time you are angry or having any emotion that feels difficult:

• Pause for a moment and pay attention. You may be having a lot of thoughts about the situation. That is fine. Let them be there.

• Pay attention for a moment to what is going on in your body. Is there tightness in your chest? Do you feel any tension in your neck, jaw, shoulders, and down your arms? Where do you feel the emotion in your body?

Reflect: Get out your journal and start writing.
Right now the way I feel anger in my body is _____ .

You don't need to do anything right now other than be aware of what is going on inside. Feel it fully. You don't need to change the situation or anything that you feel about it. You can wait to act until you feel clear. Just keep noticing what is happening inside you—not pushing it away or trying to dampen it with distractions like television or your phone.

It can be helpful to write down the things that are making you the most angry, and also what you are noticing about how you feel overall.

What happened? Describe the situation in your journal.

What about it in particular makes you angry or scared?

Present, you can handle anything. Present, you will gain perspective on how to respond (or not if you decide you don't need to). But the only way to get clear is to let yourself feel.

Breathe.

CHAPTER TWO

Mindful Yoga

Mind-Body WORKOUT

What most people think of as yoga is someone standing on one foot or getting into challenging poses. But yoga is not just a physical practice. Doing yoga creates a clear mental and emotional state as well. The word *yoga* means "union." It comes from the Sanskrit word *yuj*, meaning "to yoke or join." Yoga uses the relationship (or "union") between your mind, body, and breath to help you be present in this moment.

Obviously your mind and body (and your breathing) are connected. You can't separate one from the other. So if you feel good physically, it affects how you feel emotionally. In the same way, mental stress creates stress in your body. We've discussed how, when you are nervous or upset, your brain releases stress hormones and your muscles tighten for defense. Sometimes you can notice it right away because your hands clench and your neck and shoulders hurt. Other times, stress builds up gradually, and you don't realize it is happening until you have a headache or other pain in your body.

As we have seen, stress is a mind/body issue, so it requires a mind/body solution.

Being present therefore requires mind/body awareness. This is where yoga comes in.

Try It:

Mind/Body Connection

Feel the immediate connection between your body and your mind.

Right now, cross your arms, clench your fists, hunch your shoulders forward, round through your back, and drop your chin to your chest. How do you feel? How would you feel if you stayed like this for a long period of time?

Take a breath with your chest constricted like this. How easy or hard is it to breathe deeply?

Now press your feet into the floor, push down through your sitting bones, lengthen your spine, uncross your arms, relax your hands, roll your shoulders back gently, and open up through your chest and heart. Take a deep breath in through your nose all the way into your abdomen and let it out slowly through your mouth. How do you feel? More energized? More awake? More positive?

AAAAH

That relationship between how your body feels and how you feel emotionally is the mind/body connection. It is that simple.

Being active in any way can help you release tension and feel more at ease. Have you ever noticed how after a game or even a walk home from school you are physically tired but mentally refreshed? When you're moving, your heart pumps faster, circulating more blood and oxygen not just to the muscles, but to all the organs—including your brain. People take walks to clear their heads for exactly that reason. Moving your body can actually shift your mood.

Yoga adds another element. It is different from other forms of exercise in that it uses the relationship between your mind and your body to make it a mindfulness practice. In yoga you pay attention to what you are doing (the pose you are in) but also to how you are doing it (your focus and breathing and how your body feels right now in the pose). Your mind and body are working together for a specific purpose: being connected to the present moment.

For example, in basketball you practice to get better at passing and shooting in order to score points. That's the goal. In yoga the goal is to feel your body and breath in this moment. The idea in yoga is not to improve your eye-hand coordination or to be able to beat the other team; it is to be here now.

Most of the time we are all trying to take whatever we are doing to the next level. If you can do five pushups, you should try for seven; if you can read at an eighth-grade level, you should try for ninth. But when you are doing yoga, you are feeling what it is like to be in the pose instead of instantly moving on to the next one. Just as in other forms of mindfulness, you are being here now and paying attention to what is happening. Yoga is also a great physical exercise, but the way to get better at yoga is to get better at noticing what is happening in the moment.

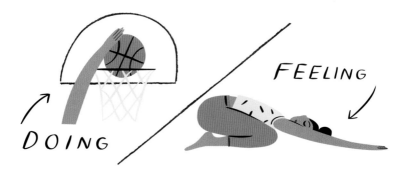

This makes yoga a non-competitive activity. It doesn't matter whether you can balance on one foot with the other extending straight up in Bird of Paradise, or perch on your knees in Crow. You are simply in this moment, in this pose, breathing in and breathing out. And if you do yoga with other people, it definitely does not matter whether they are more flexible than you are—or really what they are doing at all.

While you do this next sequence, practice matching each movement to an inhale or an exhale. This is a way to easily quiet a busy mind. This entire sequence can be done from the comfort of your chair when you want to quickly revive, relax, and feel present. (It is also a great study break.)

1 | Sit up tall, press your sitting bones into the chair, and plant your feet on the rug. Press your chest forward and stretch through your back.

2 | Now round your back, rolling your shoulders forward. (Repeat three times forward and back.)

3 | Inhale and get long through your spine, then exhale with a twist to one side. Inhale back to the midpoint, get long, and exhale with a twist to the other side. (Repeat three times.)

4 | Inhale again, and extend one arm high, stretching to the side. Exhale. Then switch sides. (Repeat three times, bending deeply on each side.)

5 | Sit up tall again and then lift one knee. Round forward to bring your forehead toward your knee. Release and switch sides. (Repeat three times.)

6 | Fall forward slowly and let your fingers touch the floor. If it is comfortable, release your neck and let your head dangle. Take three full breaths.

How do you feel?

Alignment in the Poses

The Sanskrit word for a yoga pose is *asana*. The word is also translated to mean "position" or "manner of sitting." The idea is that you are finding a relaxed "seat" in each of the poses. You are not actually sitting down in most poses, but finding your spot, your resting place, where you are comfortable. You want to look for a way to be *firm but relaxed* in each pose. That is yoga.

When you are in a pose, pay attention to the following things:

MY HANDS ARE AWAKE.

MY EYES ARE FOCUSING ON ONE POINT.

I AM NOT DOING TOO MUCH OR TOO LITTLE.

I AM PAYING ATTENTION IN THIS MOMENT.

I AM OKAY WITH THIS MOMENT AS IT IS.

MY FEET ARE FIRM UNDERNEATH ME.

Outer Alignment: Where are your eyes, your hands, and your feet in the pose?

Inner Alignment: How is your effort, attention, and acceptance in the pose?

Eyes: Fix your eyes on one point to increase focus and help with balance.

Hands: Where do they belong in the pose? Are they pressing down or reaching high? If your hands are awake, chances are you are bringing that same energy into your whole body.

Feet: Where are your feet? Are you pressing your heels to the floor? Are you standing evenly on both soles? Your feet are often the roots in whatever pose you are doing. If they are solid, you will have a strong base in the pose.

Effort: Try to find the balance in each pose of using just the amount of effort needed—not too much and not too little. You want to show up and do your best, but also to let that be enough and not try to force or overdo anything in your practice.

Attention: If there is any goal in yoga it is to be right here in the pose—right here where life is happening. Bring your attention to whatever you are feeling in the pose, and stay in the moment.

Appreciation: When present in the moment, you can accept and even appreciate what is right here, right now. If you can touch your head to your knee, you appreciate that; if you can't keep your balance in Airplane, you appreciate that too and are relaxed about it. As with all mindfulness practices, you do your best to stay open to whatever is happening in this moment without judging it.

Habits of the Mind in Yoga

You can easily fall into a negative mind (*My body can't do this*), a stuck mind (*I've never been athletic*), or a busy mind (*Where is my phone?*) while in a yoga pose. There is pretty much a guarantee that your mind will move around quite a bit. Your job is to be in the pose, breathe, and just notice how it feels. Notice where your mind is going, and bring your attention back to your hands, to your feet, to where you are focusing your eyes, and to your breathing. As with all mindfulness practices, when you notice that your attention has wandered, bring it back to the present without making it a big deal. As we've seen, those thought patterns are part of having a human mind. These mindful movement practices help strengthen the parts of the brain that regulate your emotions and problem-solving skills. Your focused effort here keeps that reactive "lizard brain" from taking control now and in other situations in your life as well.

Try another exercise to feel the immediate connection between your mind and body. (This one is amazing.)

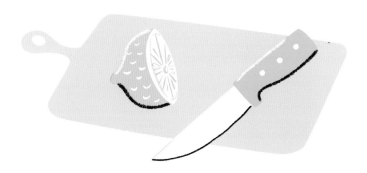

Try It:

The Lemon Experiment

Here's an exercise that lets you feel the immediate connection between your mind and body. It will require some active imagination.

Sit comfortably and be sure you won't be interrupted for the next sixty seconds.

Imagine that you are in your kitchen.

You go to the refrigerator and pull out a ripe, juicy, bright yellow lemon.

You bring it to a cutting board and get out a sharp knife.

You slice it in half—*thunk*—and immediately smell that strong, pungent, citrusy scent.

You cut it into quarters.

Take one quarter between your thumb and pointer finger.

Lift it to your mouth.

And take a big bite.

Notice: Did you at any point start to feel your mouth water with saliva, the way you would if you really bit into a lemon? Maybe it happened even before you put the imaginary lemon to your lips. Maybe you feel it right now. That is how powerful our mind/body connection is. Simply imagining the circumstances can create an actual physical response in your body.

When you practice the balance of being *firm but relaxed* on your yoga mat, it becomes easier to do it off your mat as well. Yoga builds skills that you can use when you are in other situations that require your calm focus. You experiment with how much effort is necessary to be in the posture, where to be strong, and where to relax. Then you take that same attention and awareness, that *mindfulness*, into other situations. That is how the practice of yoga then translates into all areas of your life.

*My feet are planted firmly
on the ground.*

My shoulders are back.

I am awake through my hands.

I am breathing slowly and evenly.

*I am balanced, strong,
and confident.*

I can do this.

*My feet are planted firmly
on the ground.*

My shoulders are back.

I am awake through my hands.

I am breathing slowly and evenly.

*I am balanced, strong,
and confident.*

I can do this.

The Most Important Pose

Savasana, relaxation pose, may look as if you're just lying there, but it is actually much more valuable. After moving through a series of poses, this specific rest period allows the body to return to a normal heart rate and body temperature. The stillness in this pose gives the body a chance to rejuvenate and restore its equilibrium. But for some people, being still for even five minutes of relaxation can feel impossible. Savasana is a great opportunity to learn how to go from doing to being. Often called the most difficult pose, it is also thought to be the most important.

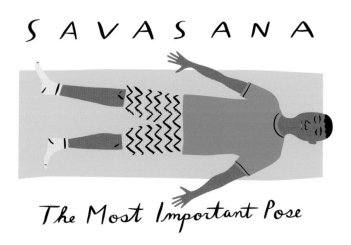

SAVASANA

The Most Important Pose

Savasana

This is a great yoga pose to do anytime for relaxation and letting go.

The physical technique of the pose is simple:

Lie flat on your back.

If you'd like, try separating your feet and then turning your toes toward one another until they touch.

Hold there for one inhale and release on the exhale.

Keep your feet gently separated.

Relax your arms along your sides, palms facing up.

Close your eyes.

Then the hard part:

Relax your whole body and let everything become still.

Focus on your natural breathing.

Stay here for three to seven minutes.

Stay as long as it takes you to feel relaxed.

Safety Review

In yoga, you are always working on balancing effort and ease in every pose. If you don't feel anything at all, you are not getting the benefits of being in the pose. But if you push too hard, you will feel strain and possibly injure yourself.

Absolutely nothing in yoga should hurt. Find the balance. Listen to your own body and make decisions about what feels good to you. What matters is the *attitude* you bring to the pose, not how flexible you are or how strong you are or how *anything* you are.

Remember: Yoga is non-competitive; you are not pushing yourself to go more deeply into the pose. If you want to improve something, improve your level of focus.

When yoga starts I always feel kind of tired, like why am I doing this, but by the end it all comes together and my whole body feels better. I feel refreshed like I hit a restart button on all my muscles. I am relaxed, but I have more energy after yoga.

—Dylan, age 11

Doing yoga in my room calms me down and gets me to a place where I can figure things out. Even if a problem is not fixed, after yoga I feel like it will be. I feel more confident. When I am lying on the floor in Savasana I feel loose, calm, energized, and accomplished.

—Jasmine, age 14

YOGA TOOL KIT

Five-minute yoga flows for every moment of your day

Each of these sequences can be done on its own or combined to create a complete thirty-minute yoga workout. It's best to do these on a yoga mat or a thick rug.

Waking Up
WELL
ENERGIZE

Try this first thing in the morning or any time you need it.

Breathe

- Sit up comfortably on your knees.
- Inhale as you lift your hands out to the side and up over your head.
- Exhale and bring your hands back to your sides.
- Repeat five times.

Child Pose

- Press back and rest onto your heels.
- Bring your head to the floor with your arms out in front of you.
- Relax.
- Inhale and exhale (five times).

Cat Tilt

- Inhale and look up, dropping your stomach toward the ground and curving your spine.
- Exhale and look toward your knees, arching your spine.
- Repeat five times.

Table Top

- Stay on your hands and knees.
- Inhale and kick your right leg back and up behind you. Look up.
- Exhale while bending your knee and bringing it gently toward your forehead. Touch your knee to your head if you can.
- Repeat five times and then switch to the left leg.

Balancing Table Top

- Rest on your hands and knees.
- Extend your right arm forward and your left leg back.
- Get long through your spine.
- Hold for five breaths.
- Switch sides: Extend your left arm forward and your right leg back.
- Hold for five breaths.

Downward Dog

- Press your palms down. Press your heels toward the floor. Lift your hips high.
- Hold for five breaths.
- Walk your feet up to your hands.
- Bend your knees.
- Roll up to standing.

Standing Mountain

- Roll your shoulders back, lengthen your spine, and lift your heart.
- Focus on one point in front of you.
- Breathe.

Sun Breath

- Inhale your hands out to the sides and up.
- Exhale your hands back down.
- Repeat five times.

Volcano

- On tiptoes, inhale your hands over your head.
- Reach high and balance.
- Breathe. Hold for two breaths.

Extended Bend (Ski Jumper)

- Bend your knees.
- Extend your hands behind you, palms facing down.
- Hold for five breaths.

Chair Pose

- Keep your knees bent.
- Extend your arms over your head.
- Focus on one point.
- Hold for five breaths.

Mountain Pose

- Stand tall.
- Press down through your feet and extend your spine.
- Gently press palm to palm.

Repeat the Sun Breath through Mountain Pose sequence three times, taking just one breath per movement.

Building
CONFIDENCE
STRENGTHEN

Mountain Pose

- Stand tall and roll your shoulders back.
- Press down through your feet and lengthen your spine.
- Gently press palm to palm.

Downward Dog

- Roll forward and walk your feet behind you. Press your palms down.
- "Walk your dog": Bend your knees and heels toward the floor side to side to loosen up through your legs.
- Press your heels down toward the floor.
- Hold for five breaths.

Forward Lunge

- Bring your right foot forward into a lunge.
- Balance with your back heel off the floor and extend your hands over your head.
- Hold for five breaths.
- Bring your right hand to the ground. (You can modify by bringing your back knee to the floor.) Raise your left hand high over your head.
- Switch legs and repeat. Hold for five breaths.

Downward Dog

- Hold for five breaths.

Warrior II

- Raise your right foot high and bring it forward into a lunge.
- Flatten your left foot on the floor behind you.
- Bend your right knee.
- Raise your arms up over your head and open wide to the sides.
- Focus your eyes on a point in front of you.
- Hold for five breaths.

Downward Dog

- Hold for five breaths.
- Switch sides (left leg forward).
- Hold for five breaths.

Warrior III

- Start in Mountain Pose.
- Focus on one point.
- Lift your right foot behind
  you and balance with your arms
  behind you, palms facing down. (This is called
  Airplane Pose.)
- Keep your chest lifting and your spine long.
- Hold for three breaths. Then bring your arms out in front
  of you. Balance. (This is Warrior III.)
- Hold for two breaths.
- Switch sides and repeat.

Tree Pose

- Lengthen through your spine.
- Rest your left foot on your right
  ankle or above the knee.
- Focus on one point and find
  your balance.
- Lift your arms out to the sides
  and then up over your head.
- Hold for five breaths.
- Switch sides and repeat.

Taming TENSION
R E L A X

Seated Pose with Goal Post Arms

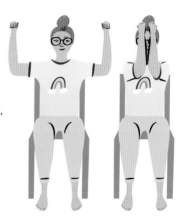

- Hold your arms as if they are goal posts. Inhale and pull your arms back.
- Exhale and round your shoulders, bringing your arms forward, elbows toward each other (touching if you can).
- Repeat five times.

Arm Twist

- Bend your right elbow and pull it to your chest. Rest your right hand on your left shoulder. Bring your left hand to hug the elbow toward your chest and deepen the stretch.
- Hold for three breaths.
- Bend your left elbow and pull it to your chest. Rest your left hand on your right shoulder. Bring your right hand to hug the elbow toward your chest and deepen the stretch.
- Hold for three breaths.
- Repeat on both sides.

Extended Arm Twist

- Bend your right elbow behind your head and place your left hand on your right elbow.
- Hold for three breaths.
- Bend your left elbow behind your head and place your right hand on your left elbow.
- Hold for three breaths.
- Repeat on both sides.

Table Top with Thread the Needle Pose

- Inhale and lift your right hand up and over your head. Keep your eye on your right hand's thumb.
- Exhale and bring your hand back down and "thread the needle" under your left arm.
- You can stay here or bring your right shoulder to the ground for a deeper tension release.
- You can stay here or extend your left hand high.
- Hold for three breaths.
- Switch sides.

Upward Dog

- Press your palms into the floor.
- Roll your shoulders back.
- Lift your legs and thighs off the floor.
- Focus on one point.
- Inhale and exhale (three times).

Child Pose

- Press back and rest onto your heels.
- Bring your head to the floor with your arms out in front of you.
- Relax.
- Inhale and exhale (three times).

On the next inhale move into Upward Dog, and then press back into Child Pose on the exhale. Alternate back and forth for five breaths.

Seated Twist

- Bring your right hand to your left knee.
- Twist your spine all the way to the left and place your left hand behind you.
- Inhale and exhale and twist a little more.
- Switch sides
- Repeat two times in each direction.

Neck Release

- Bring your right ear toward your right shoulder.
- Use your right hand on your head to gently stretch your neck.
- Extend your left palm toward the floor.
- Hold for three breaths.
- Switch sides and repeat.
- Repeat again on each side.

Feeling
OVERWHELMED
DE—STRESS

Energizing Breath

- Stand in Mountain Pose and bend gently through your knees.
- Inhale and sweep your hands up.
- Exhale forcefully and swing your arms back.
- Repeat quickly five times.

Body Twist

- Twist your body from side to side (lifting your back heel).
- Let your arms swing all the way around to your back and shoulders.
- Twist back and forth (five times each side).

Airplane into Eagle

- Start in Mountain Pose.
- Focus on one point.
- Lift your right foot behind you and balance with your arms behind you, palms facing down.

- Keep your chest lifting and your spine long.
- Hold for three breaths.
- Bring your right arm under your left arm.
- Bring your right knee over your left knee.
- Hold for three breaths.
- Switch sides and repeat from Airplane Pose.

Standing Half Moon

- Stand with your legs together, pressing both feet evenly into the ground.
- Bring your right hand to your side and lift your left hand high. Lean to the right without causing any strain.
- Breathe and focus. Notice the long stretch down the left side of your body.
- Bring your left hand to your side. Inhale and lift your right hand high. Lean to the left.
- Breathe and focus. Notice the long stretch down the right side of your body.
- Come back to center and repeat on both sides (two times).

Let It Go

- Bring your hands up over your head.
- Bring them down, palms facing the floor, all the way to the ground.
- Bend your knees and swish your hands out to the side like you are sweeping something away.
- Repeat three times.

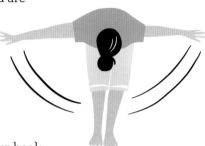

Child Pose

- Press back and rest onto your heels.
- Bring your head to the floor with your arms out in front of you.
- Relax.
- Inhale and exhale (three times).

Lying Twist

- Lie on your back.
- Bring your bent right leg over to the left for a deep twist.
- Relax.
- Inhale and exhale (three times).
- Switch sides.

Getting
READY FOR BED
R E L A X

You can use a yoga strap, bathrobe tie,
or towel for this relaxing sequence.

Seated pose

- Bring your right foot into your hands.
- Press the sole of your foot with your thumbs.
- Hold your toes and rotate them back
  and forth.
- Interlace your fingers between your toes, and
  toggle and twist gently back and forth. (If this is too
  uncomfortable, just continue to hold and rotate the toes.)
- Circle your ankle in one direction and then the other.
- Switch sides.

Lying on your back

- Hug your right knee into your chest.
- Position your right ankle across your
  left thigh (this is called Figure Four).
- Bring your arms around the left leg
  and gently pull toward your chest.
- Hold for five breaths.
- Switch legs.

Extending with strap

You'll need a strap for this pose.

- Place the strap across the ball mound of your right foot.
- Extend the right leg (while keeping the left leg on the floor).
- Hold the strap in your right hand and open the right leg to the right.
- Hold and breathe.

(See what is comfortable here.)

- Switch legs.

Extending with strap/across the body

- Switch the strap into your left hand.
- Extend the right leg across your body to the left.
- Hold and breathe comfortably.
- Straighten the right leg.
- Let go of the strap and bring the right leg to the floor slowly. (Count all the way to twenty before getting all the way down.)
- Notice the differences between the right and the left side.
- Switch sides. Start with the Figure Four.

Savasana

- End with five minutes in Savasana pose for total relaxation.

CHAPTER THREE
Mindful Breathing

CALM and AWAKE

Pay attention as your next breath comes in through your nose. Notice whether the air is cool or warm. Can you feel it move into your chest and fill your stomach? Exhale slowly.

You are always breathing, and it is easy to take it for granted. As long as you're not panting from a run, suffering from a chest cold, or (heaven forbid) choking on something, you probably don't give your breathing any thought.

And yet your breathing affects how you feel. If you are upset, one of the first things you might be told is to *"take a deep breath."* It's widely known that focusing on your breath helps you to calm down and communicate more clearly.

just breathe

You will inhale and exhale approximately 20,000 times today. Obviously breathing keeps you alive, but it can also help you to feel more relaxed in any situation. It is a connection to the present moment that is always available. When you slow down and deepen your breath, you immediately increase the health of your entire respiratory system. It is an instantaneous way to move from that agitated fight or flight mode into the rest and renew response.

Breathing is the fastest route available from anxious to calm. By changing how you are breathing, you shift from a reactive state to a receptive state. In the 1970s, Dr. Herbert Benson, a researcher at Harvard University Medical School, called that shift the "relaxation response," which describes the body's ability to slow down and increase blood flow to the brain. Slower, deeper breathing equals a calm perspective.

This connection between our breathing and our state of mind actually works both ways. If our breathing is unsteady or shallow, it can make us feel nervous and uncomfortable. Many people, even when they are not experiencing stress, unconsciously breathe shallowly: Their breathing only accesses the top of the lungs and constricts the diaphragm's range of motion. Breathing primarily in the upper chest can become a habit with some unwanted results.

Shallow Breathing

Place a hand on your stomach, right below your belly button. Take a deep breath that starts at your belly so that you can feel your hand being pushed forward. Now move your hand to the top of your chest, and try inhaling and exhaling short breaths only from that spot. It is not as relaxing as a full breath that fills your torso. Can you feel how if you continued to breathe shallowly like this it could actually make you anxious?

If you're experiencing stress or running late it is common to take shallow and quick breaths or even to stop breathing altogether for a moment. This actually makes you feel worse and decreases your ability to use your higher brain capacities, because your system has been triggered to think there is a problem. Your brain starts to go into alert/lockdown mode.

Rapidly, that basic functioning part of the brain (the lizard brain) turns to one thing only: survival.

To make matters worse, if your lungs do not get the needed full cycle of oxygenated air, they may hold on to excess carbon dioxide. Your body's response is to try to take in more oxygen, but with the carbon dioxide still there, not as much oxygen can get in, which eventually leads to that feeling of anxiousness.

The good news is that noticing and making a small change can bring instant relief.

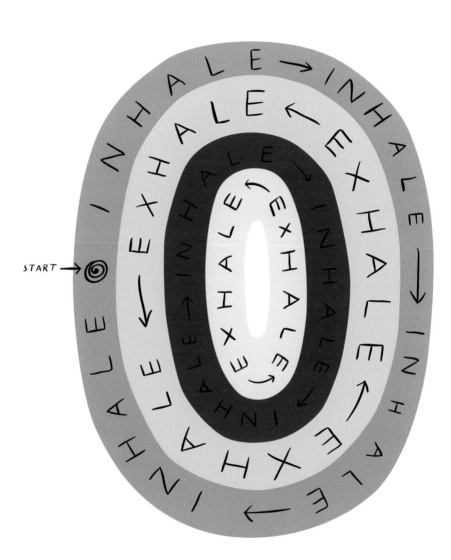

START →

Try It:

Slowing Down the Breath

Put your finger on the starting point of the outer circle, and on your next inhale trace the entire circle with your finger. As you reach the exhale point, reverse and slowly trace your way back to the start while exhaling. Move to the next circle. Take long, full breaths in and out. Repeat the process at least three times. How do you feel before and after this exercise?

It is really simple: Those deep slow breaths allow for a complete oxygen exchange in the body. A full cycle that brings in oxygen and trades out carbon dioxide regulates your blood pressure and heart rate, two crucial things that are out of balance when you feel anxiety or full-blown fear. When you are breathing deeply, your lungs fill and your belly rises. This alerts the central nervous system in the brain that everything is A-OK. Any alarm bells and flashing lights that were starting to go off inside you can be reset to a neutral state—there's no crisis here. It is truly the fastest way to feel relief. You are then able to better respond from that calm state.

Any time you pay attention to your breath, it shifts your focus to the present. In addition to relaxation and mental clarity, concentrating on your breath brings you automatically into the moment because the only breath you are ever taking is this one right now. The breath is always there as an anchor to this moment. While your mind can be like a boat, prone to drifting off on the sea of your thoughts and emotions, the breath is there to pull it back. For most people, the mind is floating off constantly. But pausing to feel the physical sensation of your next breath as it moves in and out brings you immediately back to here and now. That shift from distracted to aware is literally only one breath away.

She took a breath in and let it go.

Try It:

Sit comfortably.

On your next inhale try counting slowly 1, 2, 3.

Pause.

Exhale slowly, counting 1, 2, 3.

Inhale 1, 2, 3.

Pause.

Exhale 1, 2, 3.

Do you see how when you are focused on the breath, you are focused on the present moment?

When I focus on breathing I inhale and it feels like I am filling up with something good, and when I exhale I feel more calm.

—Kai, age 11

I like the breathing exercises because no one knows I am doing them. If I feel nervous because I have to do something in front of the class, I can take slow breaths (1, 2, 3, 4 in and 1, 2, 3, 4 out) and I feel stronger inside.

—Riya, age 12

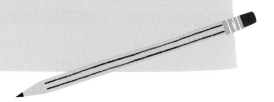

BREATHING TOOL KIT

Try these breathing techniques to give yourself a stress release or energy boost any time you need it. Each of these exercises is also a mindfulness tool. You can use the breath to connect to the present moment—immediately.

FULL ABDOMINAL BREATHING

Full abdominal breathing is our natural state when relaxed. Look at animals and babies and how their stomachs rise and fall when calm. If you pay attention, you may find that at times you are holding in your stomach instead of letting it rise and fall with the breath. Filling your abdomen fully with breath may not be the "look" we are going for, but actually it should be. The benefit of focusing on full abdominal breathing is that you activate that calm internal state (no matter what is going on).

- Place your hand on your abdomen.
- On your next inhale, breathe in slowly, expanding your stomach so it makes your hand rise up.
- Exhale and release all of the air slowly.
- Repeat. (If you don't feel any effects yet, try three more).

THREE-PART BREATH

This is a great breath for regulating a full exchange of oxygen and carbon dioxide in the body. It is also very calming.

Sit comfortably, and start by placing your hand at your belly with your thumb just underneath your belly button.

As you inhale, imagine bringing the breath all the way to your palm, and fill your lower abdomen.

As you exhale, release all of the breath.

Now bring your other hand just above your belly button.

Notice on the next inhale how you can move the bottom hand and then the top hand as you fill with breath. Exhale completely.

Take the bottom hand and bring it to your chest.

Feel on the next inhale how the breath moves into the lower abdomen, up through the torso, and into the upper chest. Exhale completely.

That is three-part breathing, and it is a great cure for nervous upper chest breathing that does not support your system to operate at its best.

RECLINING ABDOMINAL BREATHING

This is a very relaxing breath. Doing this for even sixty seconds can leave you feeling calmer and lighter.

Lie down on your back.

Rest one hand on your abdomen.

Breathe naturally.

On your next inhale, feel your whole torso fill with breath all the way down into your stomach so that your hand rises.

As you exhale, release all of the air. You should feel your hand move down.

Inhale, bringing the breath all the way into the hand and feeling it rise.

Exhale, releasing all of the air and feeling your hand sink down as your abdomen relaxes.

Try placing one hand on your chest as you breathe.

You should feel more movement in the hand on your stomach; that is what moves if you are taking full breaths.

AWARENESS OF THE BREATH

Inhale, and follow the breath in through your nose as it fills to expand your torso. Think to yourself: *When I breathe in, I know I am breathing in.*

Exhale, and follow the release of breath out through your nose. Think to yourself: *When I breathe out, I know I am breathing out.*

That's it. That is using the breath as an anchor to the present moment, and it is available anytime.

Why think *I know I am breathing in* and *I know I am breathing out*? Isn't that incredibly obvious? Well, yes and no. Are you present when you breathe? Saying it to yourself is a way to practice paying attention to what is happening in this moment, now.

OCEAN BREATH

In yoga specifically, practitioners often use "ujjayi" breath, or "ocean sounding breath," to calm and focus in the poses. It can also help to clear your nasal passages. It is great for any time, but takes a little practice. (This breath is also sometimes called "Darth Vader Breath" for reasons that will be obvious as you try it.)

Begin practicing this breath by imagining you have a mirror in front of you. Cup your hand and hold it near your mouth.

Inhale, and as you exhale, fog the mirror.

Try that two times.

Now imagine that there is a mirror in the back of your throat.

On your next inhale, with your mouth open, fog the mirror at the back of your throat. (You will start to hear the beginning of that "ocean sound.")

Try that two times.

Next, try making the fogging breath but with your mouth closed. It can seem a little odd at first, but after a bit you will get the hang of it.

Inhale.

Exhale.

FINGER BREATH

This is a useful exercise at times when you feel overwhelmed or frustrated and want to settle down. Notice if you feel impatient going through each breath. Just pay attention to that feeling—see how long it lasts as you focus on your breathing.

Clench one hand into a fist.

Squeeze it tight.

Now, take one deep breath in and one long breath out, and release your thumb from the fist.

Next, take one deep breath in and one long breath out, and release your index finger.

Take one deep breath in and one long breath out, and release your middle finger.

Take another deep breath in and another long breath out, and release your ring finger.

Finally, take one last deep breath in and one last long breath out, and release your pinkie.

REJUVENATING "WAKE UP" BREATH

This energizing breath works in seconds to make you feel awake! This breath involves three quick inhalations through your nose and a long exhalation through your mouth. It is very effective. Start slowly to get a sense of matching the breath and the movement, and then speed it up when you're ready.

- Stand tall, with your feet hip-width apart, arms by your sides.
- Let your knees gently bend.
- For your first inhale, bring your arms straight out in front of you, parallel to the earth.
- Then inhale again as you bring your hands out to the sides.
- Take your third inhale while swinging your arms up over your head.
- Exhale and let your arms swing down as you bend your knees and fold forward with a long *haaaa* sound.
- Repeat.

DANDELION BREATH

This breath is just like making a wish on a dandelion.

Cup your hand in front of your mouth.

Inhale through the nose.

Blow out through the mouth as if you could scatter all the dandelion seeds with one big gust.

Imagine that with this breath you are blowing away something that is making you tense.

Once or twice is great for releasing tension with the dandelion breath. If you feel light-headed, stop and breathe naturally.

PAUSE AND HOLD

Extending your inhale and exhale is a natural way to slow down and make sure you are giving your mind and body all of the oxygen needed. It is extremely relaxing.

Breathe normally for a moment as you prepare.

On your next breath, see if you can keep slowly inhaling for a count of four.

1 . . . 2 . . . 3 . . . 4

On the exhale, follow that same, slow count.

1 . . . 2 . . . 3 . . . 4

Repeat three more times.

LION'S BREATH

This breath is a great way to release anger or any other intense emotion. It is also very energizing.

Sit on your knees or in your chair.

Stick your tongue way out and lean forward, hands on knees.

Now take a deep breath in and then let it out forcefully, leaning forward, tongue out.

Say "Aahhhhhhh."

Repeat two more times.

CHAPTER FOUR
Mindful Meditation

Being Still
WITH SKILL

Sitting still and letting your thoughts come and go while you stay present for a period of time is another way to practice mindfulness. It is another way to train the mind to be here now. You practice paying attention when you are already still and quiet, so that you are better at being present (or noticing when you're not) during the busier, more chaotic moments in your day.

Watching your thoughts is a weird concept. Usually you don't think much about what is going on inside your head; it just happens and you respond. Scientists claim that a person has about 50,000 to 70,000 thoughts per day. As you have seen, a lot of those are on a kind of auto-loop—worried or frustrated thoughts about the same things over and over, planning the same things over and over, etc. There is necessary, helpful thinking, and there is a whole lot of thinking that probably does not serve you.

You can react to your thoughts like a dog chasing its tail with no end, or you can learn to let thoughts move through and to note them without becoming lost in them. They can seem very real, but still they are just thoughts. The more you practice meditating, the better you get at watching them come and go.

Seated meditation is a skill that requires honing. In soccer or volleyball you might do passing or serving drills; you work on one specific skill so you are better at it during the game. Well, sitting quietly and noticing your thoughts is the skill in this case; everything else in your life is game time.

Researchers at Harvard University found that meditating has a positive effect on the brain even when subjects are not meditating. People who regularly spend time in meditation show increased brain capacity for memory, empathy, focus, and the ability to "turn down" distractions.

In meditation, you sit still and notice as your thoughts come in, and then you let them move on through without holding on to them. It is like being on a train platform, with your thoughts arriving and departing the station all day long. When you are sitting still in meditation, you are working on letting them depart without you. You will find that often you get on one of the "thought trains" without realizing it and you're speeding along to a new destination. Then, gently you notice and return to the platform. Your thoughts will continue to arrive; you are practicing hopping on fewer of them.

Try It:

Being Still with Skill (Three-Minute Meditation)

Set a timer for three minutes.

*For all of the Try It and Tool Kit exercises
in this chapter, read the instructions in advance
so that you can then close your eyes while you try them.*

Find a comfortable way to sit. You are upright, but not tense and rigid. Not trying too hard, but also not trying too little.

Close your eyes and notice your breathing. Don't try to change anything about it, just breathe naturally in and out.

Now start to lengthen your inhale and your exhale. And as the next breath comes in, count 1 in your mind. On the exhale, count 2.

For the next breath in, count 3. On the exhale, count 4. Pay attention to taking a long breath in and letting a long breath out.

Keep counting each breath until you get to 10. Then repeat the count.

DISTRACTIONS

If your mind wanders before you get to 10, simply notice that it happened and begin again at 1. (It is more accurate to say *when* your mind wanders.)

Getting to 10 is not the goal; bringing

your attention back to the breath is. That is the practice.

When you hear the timer, slowly open your eyes.

It is perfectly fine if you only noticed once during the three minutes that your thoughts were wandering. Some people never notice, so doing it even once is great. To stay in seated meditation definitely requires patience and a calm and kind acceptance of whatever is happening. It takes a lot of practice.

Any discussion of seated meditation has to include talking about being uncomfortable. It is normal to be physically uncomfortable, particularly if you try it for longer periods. It is also normal to be uncomfortable with your thoughts.

Physical Discomfort

While sitting in meditation you are trying to find a balance of effort and ease. You want to sit in a way that requires some effort (perhaps not leaning back against a couch, for example) but also allows a feeling of ease throughout your body. You want to be in your body in a way that is similar to the *calm and awake* approach of mindfulness and the *firm but relaxed* approach of yoga. Imagine (or actually take) a piece of paper and crumple it up in your hand. Really squeeze it tight. If you held it like that for a while, the pointy parts of the paper would press into your palm and it would become uncomfortable. Then imagine (or try) putting no effort into it so that the crumpled piece of paper just falls to the floor. What you want to find is the right amount of effort in which you are not holding too tight or too loose. You are holding your body the way you hold that piece of paper. You are not letting it fall, but also not crushing it tight. That is the amount of effort you want to bring into your whole body as you sit. Even if it is just for one minute.

Try It:

Effort and Ease

Right now, find the seated position that is best for you. You can either sit on the floor or on a chair. You will be less likely to fall asleep if you can engage your body in this simple way:

Imagine there is a string attached to the top of your head, pulling you toward the ceiling and lengthening your spine. Gently roll your shoulders back so your chest feels open and not constricted in any way. You are using your muscles to be upright, but you are not tense. Imagine that crumpled piece of paper. Find that middle point.

You want your hips above your knees for maximum comfort, so if you are on the floor it may make sense to sit on a cushion or pillow (or several). You may also need to put a blanket or cushion under your calves to make your knees feel more comfortable. A chair is also a great option and limits knee strain.

If you are physically uncomfortable while meditating, it is fine to shift a leg or find a new way to sit. It is common have a foot fall asleep. Just figure out what works for you.

Now, see how well this position works for you. Follow the steps of the three-minute meditation on page 106.

Mental Discomfort

For most people, getting still and paying attention to what they are thinking doesn't initially feel so great. At first it can actually be the opposite of relaxing to be aware of your thoughts. Most likely you will notice a lot of the regular habits of the mind (negative, stuck, and distracted) come up quickly. You may find that you are rehashing something frustrating that happened with your brother earlier in the day. Or that you are feeling nervous about a math test that is coming later in the week. You may find that you've just redecorated your room in your mind or created a packing list for your camping trip.

The good news is that this is kind of the point. You get better at noticing those patterns of discomfort and distraction in your thinking, and then they don't have so much power over you. When you are on auto-pilot, those thoughts run the show from the background. Without awareness, you react to thoughts and feelings you may not even realize you're having. This is where meditation is so helpful. You get to see those habits and patterns very clearly.

You are working on new habits and behaviors. When you are in a class, for example, you have learned how to act. If something funny happens while you're taking a test, you don't burst out laughing; if you are hungry, you don't rush out to get food before the bell rings. In meditation, you are learning this same kind of impulse control and delayed gratification to manage how you react to your own thoughts. But instead of following a teacher's rules, you are making choices that impact how you yourself feel.

So, if it feels uncomfortable to pay attention to what you are thinking without just reacting, you are actually right where you should be. It is challenging for everyone, and it does get easier with practice. It can be hard to tell the difference between mentally working out a solution to an issue and just repetitive worry. Even short amounts of time spent being quiet help you feel the difference.

But sitting still even for three to five minutes may feel boring or irritating at the beginning. You may find yourself wondering "what's the point?" Again, you are not alone. This is probably the most common response to meditation early on. It feels so counterintuitive to "do nothing." We always think we should be *doing*, and yet *being* has many proven benefits. Studies show that time spent in meditation supports the brain's functioning in the way that sleep does for the rest of the body. It improves your ability to think creatively, have a positive attitude, and even multitask effectively.

"Don't just do something, Sit there".

— SYLVIA BOORSTEIN

Naming Thoughts

Meditation is not a tool for stopping your thoughts. Instead, it is a way to develop a better understanding of the way your mind works. The skill you are developing in meditation is the ability to "come back" when you realize your mind has gone a million miles away. When you are meditating for even short periods, it can be very helpful to use the tool of naming, or labeling, thoughts. Imagine you are on the side of a river, watching boats go by. (This is similar to the image of the trains in the station.) The boats are your thoughts, and as they pass, you name them. You see them for what they are, label them, and let them go. The boat of planning, the boat of worry, the boat of boredom, the boat of doubt, etc.

You are not making a big deal about any of them. You are just seeing them for what they are—thoughts—and letting them move on by. Many of them may just be labeled THINKING. Don't worry about getting the labels right; just noticing each new thought is the idea.

"This isn't working." (Doubt)

"I have to call Noah." (Planning)

"I think I left my shirt at Ella's." (Worry)

At times, you will get on one of the boats for a while. That is fine. Whenever you realize you are drifting away in a thought, just name it and let it continue on down the river. (It doesn't matter whether you use boats, trains, clouds, or just words in your mind. Choose an image that works for you.)

Try It:

Naming Thoughts

Set your timer for two minutes and get into a comfortable seat. Close your eyes. (Remember your balance of effort and ease and the crumpled paper.)

Take a deep breath in and let a long breath out.

Pay attention to your breath, following the inhalation in and the exhalation out through your body.

Before you know it, thoughts will be passing by.

Your job is to notice even one of them and label it. Again, don't get caught up in what the label is; just notice that you are thinking. When you notice a thought, give it a label and gently bring your attention back to your breath.

When the timer goes off, slowly open your eyes. Relax.

How did it go?

Once you start noticing, it is amazing how many thoughts will come by to offer you a ride. The practice is not stopping them—you can't—or pushing them away. You are learning to let them pass by. Your thoughts, while important, are just thoughts. They are the running commentary but they are not the final word on what is real and happening in this moment.

Now is the only moment that exists.

What is real now is the feeling of your inhale and exhale. Yes, you have a lot of images and ideas moving through your mind, some helpful, some not, and they don't all need to receive a big reaction from you. If you are present, you will know which thoughts need your attention and which are just a part of the parade endlessly drifting past.

Gentleness is key. You need to bring that same level of curiosity and relaxed kindness toward yourself in meditation that you bring to all mindfulness practices. Working with your mind is like training a puppy. You have to be patient. When a puppy forgets where it is supposed to go, you don't berate it; you understand that it is learning. You don't decide that you have a bad puppy and that it will never be able to do things well. You have faith in the process and kindly bring it back to the spot you had asked it to go in the first place. You may do that a hundred or a thousand times, and that is fine.

All of us function more effectively when we feel present. Period. The moment you have some insight into the habits of your mind, you have some choice about how you are going to react. The only time you can make a change or create something new is right now. Meditation helps you get better at being here now.

What I like about meditation is that it gives me more energy. Usually my body starts out like, why am I just going to sit still? I could be out running around, and I am just here! But after I do it, I feel like I can go with the flow more. It is almost like I avoid problems before they even happen. I don't get in trouble in school because I am just doing what I am supposed to be doing. —Eva, age 11

I meditate for two minutes before I go to sleep. I just let myself let go. Even when I have different thoughts I know I don't have to do anything about them right now, and it is really relaxing. I sleep much better.
   —Jahmai, age 12

MEDITATION TOOL KIT

These exercises help to develop the habit of being here now. We can notice when our minds are somewhere else and gently bring them back to this moment.

A Note about Timers: Timers are very helpful in meditation, particularly when you are new to sitting. It may be near impossible to "simply sit" without the structure of a specific amount of time. Use a timer for each of these exercises so that you don't have to spend time checking the clock. (You may find you peek anyway, which is fine and normal.)

Noticing the Point

Sit with a balance of effort and ease.

Set your timer for three minutes.

Now bring your attention to the point in your body where you feel the breath begin: right at the tip of your nose. Bring all of your awareness to that point on each inhalation. Keep coming back to that simple point throughout your meditation.

Labeling Meditation

Find a comfortable seat where you can feel the balance of effort and ease in your body.

Set your timer for five minutes.

Close your eyes and bring your attention to your breath. Feel your inhale and feel your exhale.

You may notice that you quickly head off into thinking, planning, worrying, doubting. You may find that you feel tired or hungry.

Whatever you feel, when you realize it, notice it, label it, and go back to paying attention to your inhale and your exhale.

Remember: Patience is key. You may only notice one thought the whole time.

123 Counting Breath Meditation

Find a comfortable seat where you can feel the balance of effort and ease in your body.

Set your timer for five minutes.

Close your eyes and bring your attention to your breath.

Take a breath in and out and count 1.

Take a breath in and out and count 2.

Take a breath in and out and count 3.

Keep going until you reach 10. Most likely, you will lose track, and that is fine. Gently bring your attention back to the breath and start over.

(The variation is to inhale 1 and exhale 2. Just do whichever feels more comfortable.)

Kindness Meditation

This ancient technique for developing kindness has modern-day applications. Research shows that practicing positive thoughts has a direct impact on how you feel about yourself and your life.

Take a comfortable seat balancing effort and ease.

Notice the inhale and exhale of your breath.

The first part of the practice is kindness toward yourself. You repeat silently to yourself:

May I be safe.
May I be healthy.
May I be happy.

You can try saying it three times slowly before moving on.

Now, think about someone you love. This should be someone who brings a positive feeling when you think of them. Picture this person clearly in your mind, silently give them the same wish, repeated three times:

May you be safe.
May you be healthy.
May you be happy.

If you want to build on the practice, bring to mind someone you know but don't have a strong feeling about one way or another. Practice saying to them:

May you be safe.
May you be healthy.
May you be happy.

You can also try this three times.

Here comes the final level of this exercise. Choose someone you have difficult feelings about. This could be someone you don't like, or someone you are angry at. When you think of this person, you do not have a positive association. Here, you stay connected to your breath, and work slowly through the words three times, noticing what comes up. Keep breathing. This is advanced.

May you be safe.
May you be healthy.
May you be happy.

PEACE.

Finger Meditation

This is a quick and easy way to do a mini-meditation in the moment.

Simply touch your thumb to each finger on your hand, saying silently:

Peace begins with me.

You can also replace the word *peace* with anything that feels important to you:

Change begins with me.

Calm begins with me.

Or find another expression of it:

I am completely calm.

I am so strong.

I am confident here.

I am confident now.

Concentration Meditation (Object)

Sometimes focusing on an image (like a flower or a candle) either in your mind or in front of you can be helpful. For this exercise, try choosing an actual object. Choose something you like to look at but that does not have any words written on it. Get into a comfortable seat and set the object where you can see it easily.

Set a timer for three minutes.

Keep your eyes gently open and look at your object.

Breathe normally and keep your attention on the object. Notice everything you can about it without actually picking it up.

You may find that even though your eyes are open, you forget what you are looking at from time to time as other thoughts take over. That is fine. Just gently bring your attention back to your object.

Concentration Meditation (Word)

Sometimes focusing on a word can be helpful. Choose a simple word to repeat that gives you something to come back to when your thoughts wander (similar to counting breaths).

Get into a comfortable seat and try the following exercise using the word *relax*:

Re-lax.

As you breathe in silently say *Re*.

As you breathe out silently say *lax*.

Continue with a timer for three minutes, coming back to *Re-lax* when you lose focus.

Meditative Body Scan

Sit comfortably and close your eyes. Breathe naturally. No timer is needed for this exercise.

Bring your attention to the soles of your feet. Just notice them. Take your time.

Now bring that attention to the tops of your feet,

then to your ankles,

then your calves,

your shins,

your knees . . .

Continue bringing your attention up through your body until you reach the top of your head.

Open your eyes.

Color Meditation

Set your timer for three minutes.

Sit comfortably and close your eyes.

Breathe naturally.

Imagine on your next inhale that your breath is filling your whole body with the color blue.

Imagine this color filling you to the edges of your body.

As you exhale, imagine that your whole body is breathing out all the color.

Inhale—breathe in vibrant blue.

Exhale—release vibrant blue.

Repeat.

Walking Meditation

There are forms of walking meditation that focus on making very slow, deliberate, mindful movements. For this exercise, you are bringing your attention and awareness to your senses as you move at a regular pace. Take a ten-minute walk, or decide to try this next time you are going somewhere by foot.

Use your senses to move through the following exercise.

First, notice how your body feels walking. Notice your feet hitting the ground, and how your legs, hips, and arms are moving.

Notice your breath. How is it changing depending on your pace and the terrain? Pay attention.

Notice the air or wind on your skin. Is it cool? Warm? Refreshing or clammy?

Now pay attention to what you can hear. Bring all of your awareness to the sounds around you. Notice whether they are natural or man-made.

Now focus on what you see. What is the light like, and is it different in different places? What colors stand out to you?

CHAPTER FIVE

5-DAY
Mindfulness
Challenges

Now you know that adding mindfulness into your day is as simple as noticing your next breath or the feeling of your body in your chair. These Five-Day Skill-Building Challenges are how-to guides that give you a plan and structure for starting to make mindfulness a regular part of your day. Five days is a short commitment, but long enough for you to feel the positive effects.

Each five-day segment is designed to work within your already-full schedule of school, homework, extracurriculars, friends, and family. Some of the activities are specific to the time of day (first thing in the morning or before you go to sleep), but most are for you to do at any moment that works for you. Just do them at some point during that specific twenty-four-hour period. The idea is that you can bring these mindfulness practices easily into your day-to-day routines with great results. A little goes a long way.

Remember: You are trying something new. Be patient with yourself. Pay attention to the thoughts you have that get in your way: *Why do this? I don't have time. I forgot to do today's exercises, so I won't do it at all this week.* Instead of reacting to those thoughts, practice mindfulness: Notice what you feel, and let it be. Do a Five-Day Challenge. Then see how you feel.

Find out for yourself.

As always, be present and enjoy the moment!

THE BEST AND MOST BEAUTIFUL THINGS IN THE WORLD CANNOT BE SEEN OR EVEN TOUCHED— THEY MUST BE FELT WITH THE HEART.

—Helen Keller

RELAX AND RESET

Note: In this Five-Day Challenge and the following ones as well, the yoga flow will build throughout the five days. You might find that the beginning of the day is the best time for this portion of the challenge, or you might feel less rushed when you get home from school.

Energizing Breath

- Stand with hands by your sides.
- Bend gently through your knees.
- Inhale and sweep your hands up.
- Exhale forcefully and swing your arms back.
- Repeat quickly five times.

Sun Breath

- Stand comfortably.
- Bring your hands out to your sides and up.
- Inhale and lift your arms high.
- Exhale and bring your hands together at the center of your heart.
- Make your movements slow and smooth.
- Match your breath and movement.
- Repeat five times.

Body Twist

- Twist your body from side to side (lifting your back heel).
- Let your arms swing all the way around to your back and shoulders.
- Twist back and forth (five times per side).

Focused Breathing Meditation

- Set your timer for two minutes.
- As you breathe in, silently say *Re*
- As you breathe out, silently say *lax*.
- Continue coming back to *Re-lax* when you lose focus.

Mindful Breathing

- This is a good exercise to do right before you go to sleep. Place your hand on your abdomen.
- On your next inhale, slowly breathe in, expanding your stomach so it makes your hand rise up. Notice the sensations in your body as you inhale.
- Exhale and release all of the air slowly. Be present and notice the sensations in your body as you exhale. Notice whether you can feel your whole body relax and let go a bit more with each exhale.
- Repeat. (If you don't feel any effects yet, try three more.)

Action Step: Positive Message

Take this step as early in the day as you can. Write a positive message, and post it somewhere you will see it all week. (Try using washable markers on your mirror or a sticky note on your desk.) You can use a quote you love, or one meaningful word.

"Work Hard, Do Your Part, Be Kind. And Darling,
Don't Forget There's Magic." —Leigh Standley

"Surrender your fear,
and trust your strength." —Kelly Rae Roberts

Make sure you've put this word or quote somewhere you will see it daily. Each time you see it, notice how it makes you feel. Notice your emotional and physical responses.

DAY ②

Energizing Breath

- Bend gently through your knees.
- Inhale and sweep your hands up.
- Exhale forcefully and swing your arms back.
- Repeat quickly five times.

Sun Breath

- Stand comfortably.
- Bring your hands out to your sides and up.
- Inhale and lift your arms high.
- Exhale and bring your hands together at the center of your heart.
- Make your movements slow and smooth.
- Match your breath and movement.
- Repeat five times.

Body Twist

- Twist your body from side to side (lifting your back heel).
- Let your arms swing all the way around to your back and shoulders.
- Twist back and forth (five times per side).

Airplane Pose into Eagle Pose

- Go into Mountain Pose (stand tall with arms down and palms facing forward).
- Focus on one point.
- Lift your right foot behind you and balance with your arms behind you, palms facing down.
- Keep your chest lifting and your spine long.
- Hold for three breaths.
- Bring your right arm under your left arm.
- Bring your right knee over your left knee.
- Hold for three breaths.
- Switch sides and repeat from Airplane Pose.

Focused Breathing Meditation

- Set your timer for two minutes.
- As you breathe in, silently say *Re*.
- As you breathe out, silently say *lax*.
- Continue coming back to *Re-lax* when you lose focus.

Supine Mindful Breathing

This will work well as a pre-bedtime exercise.

- Lie down on your back on the bed.
- Bring your attention to the back of your body, and feel all of the points where your body is touching the bed.

- See if you can relax your body a little more, almost as if you are melting into your bed.
- Inhale and follow the breath in through your nose as it fills to expand your torso. Think: *When I breathe in, I know I am breathing in.*
- Exhale and follow the release of breath out through your nose. Think: *When I breathe out, I know I am breathing out.*
- That's it. That is using the breath as an anchor to the present moment, and it is available anytime.

Action Step: Fresh Eyes

At some point today, take out a journal or notebook and pens or pencils. You will be drawing.

Choose something from nature that you can focus on for a few minutes. This could be a leaf or a flower, a spider's web, or even the clouds. It could be something you see on your way to school or when you go outside during the school day. (If you are doing this indoors, choose a plant, or sit by a window and pick something you see outside.)

Commit to seeing this object as if you have never seen it before. There's a movie in which a boy, raised on Mars (it's a long story), sees a horse for the first time and nearly jumps out of his seat. Can you imagine seeing a horse for the first time? Bring that level of interest and "fresh eyes" to your object. Notice everything you can about it. The color, the texture, the way it moves, and the way the light reflects on it.

Pay complete attention until you see something about it that you have not noticed before. Then take out your notebook or journal and sketch what you see. Don't worry about how it looks; focus on how your pens or pencils move on the page, and on what you are noticing about the object.

DAY ③

Energizing Breath

- Bend gently through your knees.
- Inhale and sweep your hands up.
- Exhale forcefully and swing your arms back.
- Repeat quickly five times.

Sun Breath

- Stand comfortably.
- Bring your hands out to your sides and up.
- Inhale and lift your arms high.
- Exhale and bring your hands together
  at the center of your heart.
- Make your movements slow and smooth.
- Match your breath and movement.
- Repeat five times.

Body Twist

- Twist your body from side to side
  (lifting your back heel).
- Let your arms swing all the way around
  to your back and shoulders.
- Twist back and forth (five times per side).

Airplane Pose into Eagle Pose

- Go into Mountain Pose (stand tall with arms down and palms facing forward).
- Focus on one point.
- Lift your right foot behind you and balance with your arms behind you, palms facing down.
- Keep your chest lifting and your spine long.
- Hold for three breaths.
- Bring your right arm under your left arm.
- Bring your right knee over your left knee.
- Hold for three breaths.
- Switch sides and repeat from Airplane Pose.

Standing Half Moon Pose

- Stand with your legs together, pressing both feet evenly into the ground.
- Bring your right hand to your side, and lift your left hand high.
- Lean to the right without causing any strain in your body.
- Breathe and focus. Notice the long stretch down the left side of your body.
- Inhale and bring your right hand high while placing your left hand on your side.
- Lean to the left.

- Breathe and focus. Notice the long

  stretch down the right side of your body.
- Come back to center and repeat on both sides.

Counting Breath Meditation

- Find a comfortable seat where you

  can feel the balance of effort and ease in your body.
- Set your timer for five minutes.
- Close your eyes and bring your attention to your breath.
- Take a breath in and out and count 1.
- Take a breath in and out and count 2.

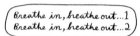

- Take a breath in and out and count 3.
- Keep going until you reach 10.

  Most likely, you will lose track, and that

  is fine. Gently bring your attention back

  to the breath and start over.

  (The variation is to inhale 1 and exhale 2.

  Just do whichever feels more comfortable.)

Finger Breath

- Clench one hand into a fist.
- Squeeze it tight.
- Now, take one deep breath in and one

  long breath out, and release your thumb from the fist.

- Next, take one deep breath in and one long breath out, and release your index finger.
- Take one deep breath in and one long breath out, and release your middle finger.
- Take another deep breath in and another long breath out, and release your ring finger.
- Finally, take one last deep breath in and one last long breath out, and release your pinkie.

Action Step: Water Exercise

The shower is a great time to practice being in the moment. Next time you take a shower, pay attention to the feeling of the beads of water on your head and skin. Notice the sensations and the temperature. Notice the smell of the soap and shampoo. Be totally present and notice everything you can.

Choose three words that describe the experience.

DAY ④

Energizing Breath

- Bend gently through your knees.
- Inhale and sweep your hands up.
- Exhale forcefully and swing your arms back.
- Repeat quickly five times.

Sun Breath

- Stand comfortably.
- Bring your hands out to your sides and up.
- Inhale and lift your arms high.
- Exhale and bring your hands together at the center of your heart.
- Make your movements slow and smooth.
- Match your breath and movement.
- Repeat five times.

Body Twist

- Twist your body from side to side (lifting your back heel).
- Let your arms swing all the way around to your back and shoulders.
- Twist back and forth (five times per side).

Airplane Pose into Eagle Pose

- Go into Mountain Pose (stand tall with arms down and palms facing forward).
- Focus on one point.
- Lift your right foot behind you and balance with your arms behind you, palms facing down.
- Keep your chest lifting and your spine long.
- Hold for three breaths.
- Bring your right arm under your left arm.
- Bring your right knee over your left knee.
- Hold for three breaths.
- Switch sides and repeat from Airplane Pose.

Standing Half Moon Pose

- Stand with your legs together, pressing both feet evenly into the ground.
- Bring your right hand to your side and lift your left hand high.
- Lean to the right without causing any strain in your body.
- Breathe and focus. Notice the long stretch down the left side of your body.
- Inhale and bring your right hand high, placing your left hand on your side.
- Lean to the left.

- Breathe and focus. Notice the long
  stretch down the right side of your body.
- Come back to center and repeat on both sides.

Let It Go

- Bring your hands up over your head.
- Bring them down, palms facing the floor,
  folding forward so your hands reach all
  the way to the ground.
- Bend your knees and swish your hands
  out to the side like you are sweeping something away.
- Repeat three times.

Child Pose

- Press back and rest onto your heels.
- Bring your head to the floor with
  your arms out in front of you.
- Relax.
- Inhale and exhale (three times).

Breathe in, breathe out...1
Breathe in, breathe out...2

Counting Breath Meditation

- Find a comfortable seat where you can feel
  the balance of effort and ease in your body.
- Set your timer for seven minutes.

- Close your eyes and bring your attention to your breath.
- Take a breath in and out and count 1.
- Take a breath in and out and count 2.
- Take a breath in and out and count 3.
- Keep going until you reach 10. Most likely, you will lose track, and that is fine. Gently bring your attention back to the breath and start over. (The variation is to inhale 1 and exhale 2. Just do whichever feels more comfortable.)

Three-Count Breathing

- Sit comfortably.
- On your next inhale try counting slowly 1, 2, 3.
- Pause.
- Exhale slowly, counting 1, 2, 3.
- Pause.
- Inhale 1, 2, 3.
- Pause.
- Exhale 1, 2, 3.
- Repeat three more times.

Action Step: Reset Button

Sometimes the best thing you can do is hit the Reset Button:
Take a break to do something you love—just because you can.

Enjoy yourself! Life will still be here when you are done.

Some suggestions:

- Take a bath
- Take a nap
- Do a body scan
- Rest in Savasana pose
- Play music that you love—
  maybe play it loud and dance!
- Cook something new
- Bake a tried-and-true favorite
- Clean your room—just making your bed and organizing
  one bookcase can make things feel more spacious
- Change your room in some way

DAY ⑤

Energizing Breath

- Bend gently through your knees.
- Inhale and sweep your hands up.
- Exhale forcefully and swing your arms back.
- Repeat quickly five times.

Sun Breath

- Stand comfortably.
- Bring your hands out to your sides and up.
- Inhale and lift your arms high.
- Exhale and bring your hands together at the center of your heart.
- Make your movements slow and smooth.
- Match your breath and movement.
- Repeat five times.

Body Twist

- Twist your body from side to side (lifting your back heel).
- Let your arms swing all the way around to your back and shoulders.
- Twist back and forth (five times per side).

Airplane Pose into Eagle Pose

- Go into Mountain Pose (stand tall with arms down and palms facing forward).
- Focus on one point.
- Lift your right foot behind you and balance with your arms behind you, palms facing down.
- Keep your chest lifting and your spine long.
- Hold for three breaths.
- Bring your right arm under your left arm.
- Bring your right knee over your left knee.
- Hold for three breaths.
- Switch sides and repeat from Airplane Pose.

Standing Half Moon

- Stand with your legs together, pressing both feet evenly into the ground.
- Bring your right hand to your side and lift your left hand high.
- Lean to the right without causing any strain in your body.
- Breathe and focus. Notice the long stretch down the left side of your body.
- Inhale and bring your right hand high, placing your left hand on your side. Lean to the left.
- Breathe and focus. Notice the long stretch down the right side of your body.
- Come back to center and repeat on both sides.

Let It Go

- Bring your hands up over your head.
- Bring them down, palms facing the floor, all the way to the ground.
- Bend your knees and swish your hands out to the side like you are sweeping something away.
- Repeat three times.

Child Pose

- Press back and rest onto your heels.
- Bring your head to the floor with your arms out in front of you.
- Relax.
- Inhale and exhale (three times).

Lying Twist

- Lie on your back.
- Bring your bent right leg over to the left for a deep twist.
- Relax.
- Inhale and exhale (three times).
- Switch sides.
- Relax on your back, arms and legs gently straight, for Savasana.

Counting Breath Meditation

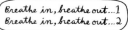

- Find a comfortable seat where you can feel the balance of effort and ease in your body.
- Set your timer for seven minutes.
- Close your eyes and bring your attention to your breath.
- Take a breath in and out and count 1.
- Take a breath in and out and count 2.
- Take a breath in and out and count 3.
- Keep going until you reach 10. Most likely, you will lose track, and that is fine. Gently bring your attention back to the breath and start over. (The variation is to inhale 1 and exhale 2. Just do whichever feels more comfortable.)

Rainbow Breath

You can do this breathing exercise sitting or standing.
- Bring your hands parallel out to your sides.
- Take a deep breath in and slowly lift your hands to meet palm to palm above your head.
- Turn your palms out and exhale back to a parallel position (creating a rainbow).
- Repeat, matching breath to movement (five times)

Action Step: Brushing Your Teeth

When you brush your teeth today, pay attention to the sensations and the temperature of the water. Feel the scrub of the bristles across your teeth and gums. Focus on the strong taste of the toothpaste. Notice every aspect of brushing your teeth. It is great practice for being in the moment.

Choose three words that describe what you noticed while doing this exercise.

Congratulations! You have completed
the **Relax and Reset** Five-Day
Mindfulness Challenge!

TRY TO BE A RAINBOW IN SOMEONE ELSE'S CLOUD.

—Maya Angelou

FEELING FANTASTIC INSIDE AND OUT

DAY ①

Seated Sun Breath

- Take a comfortable seat.
- Inhale your hands out to the side and up over your head.
- Exhale and bring your hands back to your sides.
- Repeat five times.

Child Pose

- Press back and rest onto your heels.
- Bring your head to the floor with your arms out in front of you.
- Relax.
- Inhale and exhale (five times).

Cat Tilt

- Inhale and look up, dropping your stomach toward the ground and curving your spine.
- Exhale and look toward your knees.
- Arch your spine.
- Repeat five times.

Noticing the Point

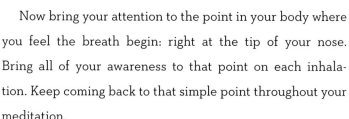

Sit with a balance of effort and ease.

Set your timer for three minutes.

Now bring your attention to the point in your body where you feel the breath begin: right at the tip of your nose. Bring all of your awareness to that point on each inhalation. Keep coming back to that simple point throughout your meditation.

If you notice a thought, label it (Thinking, Doubt, etc.) and come back to your breath.

One-Breath Mindfulness Exercise

Take a moment during your day to notice your in-breath and your out-breath. It does not need to be more complicated than that. Just check in, at some point—in math, at your locker, walking down the hall—to feel the moment. Take in one breath and let it out. See if you feel a little more focused and able to handle whatever is in front of you.

Reflect in your journal:

I paused and noticed one breath when _____.

I felt _____ .

Action Step: Gratitude

What are three things you are grateful for? These could be something obvious like your family or a friend, or anything at all that comes to mind: sunshine, a favorite food, the fact that there's a school break coming up, etc. Write them down, and take a minute or two to focus on what you've written.

DAY ②

Seated Sun Breath

- Take a comfortable seat.
- Inhale your hands out to the side
  and up over your head.
- Exhale and bring your hands back to your sides.
- Repeat five times.

Child Pose

- Press back and rest onto your heels.
- Bring your head to the floor with
  your arms out in front of you.
- Relax.
- Inhale and exhale
(five times).

Cat Tilt

- Inhale and look up, dropping your
  stomach toward the ground and curving
  your spine.
- Exhale and look toward your knees.
  Arch your spine.
- Repeat five times.

Table Top Pose

- Stay on your hands and knees.
- Inhaling, kick your right leg back and up behind you. Look up.
- Exhaling, bend your knee and bring it gently toward your forehead. (Touch knee to head if you can.)
- Repeat five times and then switch to the left leg.

Balancing Table Top

- Rest on your hands and knees.
- Extend your right arm forward and your left leg back.
- Get long through your spine.
- Hold for five breaths.
- Switch sides: Extend your left arm forward and your right leg back.
- Hold for five breaths.

Noticing the Point

Sit with a balance of effort and ease.

Set your timer for three minutes.

Now bring your attention to the point in your body where you feel the breath begin: right at the tip of your nose. Bring all of your awareness to that point on each inhalation. Keep coming back to that simple point throughout your meditation.

If you notice a thought, label it (Thinking, Doubt, etc.) and come back to your breath.

One-Breath Mindfulness Exercise

(Continue this practice from yesterday)

Take a moment during your day to notice your in-breath and your out-breath. It does not need to be more complicated than that. Just check in, at some point—in math, at your locker, walking down the hall—to feel the moment. Take in one breath and let it out. See if you feel a little more focused and able to handle whatever is in front of you.

Reflect in your journal:

I paused and noticed one breath when _____.

I felt _____ .

Action Step: Gratitude

List five things you are grateful for: Write them down. Take a minute or two to focus on what you've written.

DAY ③

Seated Sun Breath

- Take a comfortable seat.
- Inhale your hands out to the side and up over your head.
- Exhale and bring your hands back to your sides.
- Repeat five times.

Child Pose

- Press back and rest onto your heels.
- Bring your head to the floor with your arms out in front of you.
- Relax.
- Inhale and exhale (five times).

Cat Tilt

- Inhale and look up, dropping your stomach toward the ground and curving your spine.
- Exhale and look toward your knees. Arch your spine.
- Repeat five times.

Table Top Pose

- Stay on your hands and knees.
- Inhaling, kick your right leg back and up behind you. Look up.
- Exhaling, bend your knee and bring it gently toward your forehead. (Touch knee to head if you can.)
- Repeat five times and then switch to the left leg.

Balancing Table Top

- Rest on your hands and knees.
- Extend your right arm forward and your left leg back.
- Get long through your spine.
- Hold for five breaths.
- Switch sides: Extend your left arm forward and your right leg back.
- Hold for five breaths.

Downward Dog

- Press your palms down.
- Press your heels toward the floor.
- Hold for five breaths.
- Walk your feet up to your hands.
- Bend your knees.
- Roll up to standing.

Mountain Pose

- Roll your shoulders back, lengthen your spine, and lift your heart.
- Focus on one point in front of you.
- Breathe.

Noticing the Point

Sit with a balance of effort and ease.

Set your timer for five minutes.

Now bring your attention to the point in your body where you feel the breath begin: right at the tip of your nose. Bring all of your awareness to that point on each inhalation. Keep coming back to that simple point throughout your meditation.

If you notice a thought, label it (Thinking, Doubt, etc.) and come back to your breath.

Door Handle Mindfulness Exercise

Each time you enter a different room in your school, notice your hand on the door. Does it have a knob or is it a handle? Is it cold to the touch? Does it move easily or do you have to work it? Be aware of your surroundings. Practice noticing.

Reflect:

I noticed _____.

Action Step: Gratitude

List seven things you are grateful for. Try to come up with a new list—not repeating anything from your previous days' lists. Try to expand on what you appreciate. Write them down.

Take a minute or two to focus on what you're grateful for.

DAY ④

Seated Sun Breath

- Take a comfortable seat.
- Inhale your hands out to the side and up over your head.
- Exhale and bring your hands back to your sides.
- Repeat five times.

Child Pose

- Press back and rest onto your heels.
- Bring your head to the floor with your arms out in front of you.
- Relax.
- Inhale and exhale (five times).

Cat Tilt

- Inhale and look up, dropping your stomach toward the ground and curving your spine.
- Exhale and look toward your knees. Arch your spine.
- Repeat five times.

Table Top Pose

- Stay on your hands and knees.
- Inhaling, kick your right leg back and up behind you. Look up.
- Exhaling, bend your knee and bring it gently toward your forehead. (Touch knee to head if you can.)
- Repeat five times and then switch to the left leg.

Balancing Table Top

- Rest on your hands and knees.
- Extend your right arm forward and your left leg back.
- Get long through your spine.
- Hold for five breaths.
- Switch sides: Extend your left arm forward and your right leg back.
- Hold for five breaths.

Downward Dog

- Press your palms down.
- Press your heels toward the floor.
- Hold for five breaths.
- Walk your feet up to your hands.
- Bend your knees.
- Roll up to standing.

Mountain Pose

- Roll your shoulders back, lengthen your spine, and lift your heart.
- Focus on one point in front of you.
- Breathe.

Sun Breath

- Inhale your hands out to the sides and up.
- Exhale your hands back down.
- Repeat five times.

Volcano Pose

- On tiptoes, inhale your hands over your head.
- Reach high and balance.
- Breathe.

Extended Bend (Ski Jumper)

- Bend your knees.
- Extend your hands behind you, palms facing down.
- Hold for five breaths.

Chair Pose

- Keep your knees bent.
- Extend your arms over your head.
- Focus on one point.
- Hold for five breaths.

Mountain Pose

- Stand tall.
- Press down through your feet and extend your spine.
- Gently press palm to palm in front of your heart.

Take a comfortable seat balancing effort and ease.

Notice the inhale and exhale of your breath.

The first part of the practice is kindness toward yourself. Repeat silently to yourself:

May I be safe

May I be healthy

May I be happy

Say it three times slowly before moving on to a loved one.

Now think about someone you love. This should be someone who brings a positive feeling when you think of them. Picture this person clearly in your mind. Silently give them the same wish, repeated three times:

May you be safe

May you be healthy

May you be happy

Action Step: Kindness

What are two things you have done for someone else today? If you are not sure, pay attention to this question, and come back to it in twenty-four hours. What do you do for other people?

DAY ⑤

Seated Sun Breath

- Take a comfortable seat.
- Inhale your hands out to the side and up over your head.
- Exhale and bring your hands back to your sides.
- Repeat five times.

Child Pose

- Press back and rest onto your heels.
- Bring your head to the floor with your arms out in front of you.
- Relax.
- Inhale and exhale (five times).

Cat Tilt

- Inhale and look up, dropping your stomach toward the ground and curving your spine.
- Exhale and look toward your knees. Arch your spine.
- Repeat five times.

Table Top Pose

- Stay on your hands and knees.
- Inhaling, kick your right leg back and up behind you. Look up.
- Exhaling, bend your knee and bring it gently toward your forehead. (Touch knee to head if you can.)
- Repeat five times and then switch to the left leg.

Balancing Table Top

- Rest on your hands and knees.
- Extend your right arm forward and your left leg back.
- Get long through your spine.
- Hold for five breaths.
- Switch sides: Extend your left arm forward and your right leg back.
- Hold for five breaths.

Downward Dog

- Press your palms down.
- Press your heels toward the floor.
- Hold for five breaths.
- Walk your feet up to your hands.
- Bend your knees.
- Roll up to standing.

Mountain Pose

- Roll your shoulders back,
  lengthen your spine, and lift your heart.
- Focus on one point in front of you.
- Breathe.

Sun Breath

- Inhale your hands out to the sides and up.
- Exhale your hands back down.
- Repeat five times.

Volcano

- On tiptoes, inhale your hands over your head.
- Reach high and balance.
- Breathe.

Extended Bend (Ski Jumper)

- Bend your knees.
- Extend your hands behind you, palms facing down.
- Hold for five breaths.

Chair Pose

- Keep your knees bent.
- Extend your arms over your head.
- Focus on one point.
- Hold for five breaths.

Mountain Pose

- Stand tall.
- Press down through your feet and extend your spine.
- Gently press palm to palm at your heart.

Repeat the Sun Breath through Mountain Pose
sequence three times: one inhale,
one exhale per movement.

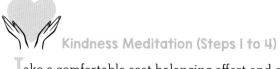

Kindness Meditation (Steps 1 to 4)

Take a comfortable seat balancing effort and ease.

Notice the inhale and exhale of your breath.

The first part of the practice is for kindness toward yourself.

Repeat silently to yourself:

> *May I be safe*
>
> *May I be healthy*
>
> *May I be happy*

Say it three times slowly before moving on to a loved one.

Now think about someone you love. This should be someone who brings a positive feeling when you think of them. Picture this person clearly in your mind. Silently give them the same wish, repeated three times:

> *May you be safe*
>
> *May you be healthy*
>
> *May you be happy*

If you want to build on the practice, bring to mind someone you know but don't have a strong feeling about one way or another. Practice saying to them:

May you be safe
May you be healthy
May you be happy

Repeat this three times.

Here comes the final level of this exercise. Choose someone you have difficult feelings about. This could be someone you don't like, or someone you are angry at. When you think of this person, you do not have a positive association. Here, you stay connected to your breath, and work slowly through the words three times, noticing what comes up. Keep breathing. This is advanced.

May you be safe
May you be healthy
May you be happy

Action Step: Body Scan (Lying down)

Read this through first, and then lie down to do the exercise. Keep the book next to you if you need to review. Once you've done this a couple of times, you won't need the book.

You can lie down on your bed or the floor. (It can be helpful to choose a harder surface like the floor, but do what is comfortable.)

• Close your eyes. Feel your breath as it comes in and out. Inhale. Exhale.

• Bring your awareness to your feet. Notice the bottoms of your feet, the tops of your feet, your toes.

• Now bring your awareness to your ankles. Notice any sensations as you shine your attention like a spotlight there.

• Bring your attention to your legs. Notice where the backs of your legs are touching the bed or the floor. Notice the sensations there as if you have never paid attention or felt this before.

• Feel your attention move to your hips.

• Let it move to your torso, your stomach, your back.

• Now shine that spotlight of attention onto your arms, and then all the way down to your hands. Be aware of each finger. Notice any sensations.

• Choose now to shift your attention to your shoulders. This is often a place of tension and stress. Just notice anything you can here. You're not trying to change anything right now—just noticing it.

• Now bring your awareness to your neck. The back of the neck, the front, the throat.

• Feel your attention move up to your face. Your jaw, your lips, your cheekbones, your nose, your eyes, your ears, your forehead, and the top of your head.

• Now bring your attention back to your breath. Inhale. Exhale.

Congratulations! You have completed
the **Feeling Fantastic Inside and Out**
Five-Day Mindfulness Challenge!

MAY
ALL OF YOUR
DREAMS SAY
"I've got this".

PERSONAL VISION

DAY ①

Mountain Pose

- Stand tall and roll your shoulders back.
- Press down through your feet and lengthen your spine.
- Gently press palm to palm at your heart.

Downward Dog

- Press your palms down.
- Bend your knees and walk your heels toward the floor
  side to side to loosen up through your legs.
- Press your heels down toward the floor.
- Hold for five breaths.

Forward Lunge

- Bring your right foot forward into a lunge.
- Balance with your back heel off the
  floor and extend your hands over your head.
- Hold for five breaths.
- Switch legs and repeat.
- Hold for five breaths.

Labeling Meditation

Find a comfortable seat where you can feel the balance of effort and ease in your body.

Set your timer for five minutes.

Close your eyes and bring your attention to your breath. Feel your inhale and feel your exhale.

You may notice that you quickly head off into thinking, planning, worrying, doubting. You may find that you feel tired or hungry.

Whatever you feel, when you realize it, notice it, label

it, and go back to paying attention to your inhale and your exhale.

Remember: Patience is key. You may only notice one thought the whole time.

Action Step: Goal-Setting

Choose a goal that you want to focus on this week. It can be as simple or challenging as you want: keeping your room clean, doing well on a math quiz, not fighting with your sister, getting a job for the summer, making it onto a team, etc.

Write it down as if it is already happening:

I am _____ .

I have _____ .

Post this goal somewhere you will see it daily. Read it aloud, then close your eyes and focus your attention on it. As clearly as you can, see yourself achieving the goal.

DAY ②

Mountain Pose

- Stand tall and roll your shoulders back.
- Press down through your feet and lengthen your spine.
- Gently press palm to palm at your heart.

Downward Dog

- Press your palms down.
- Bend your knees and walk your heels side to side to loosen up through your legs.
- Press your heels down toward the floor.
- Hold for five breaths.

Forward Lunge

- Bring your right foot forward into a lunge.
- Balance with your back heel off the floor and extend your hands over your head.
- Hold for five breaths.
- Switch legs and repeat.
- Hold for five breaths.

Downward Dog

- Hold for five breaths.

Warrior II

- Raise your right foot high and bring it forward into a lunge.
- Flatten your left foot on the floor behind you.
- Bend your right knee.
- Raise your arms up over your head and open wide to the sides.
- Focus your eyes on a point in front of you.
- Hold for five breaths.

Downward Dog

- Hold for five breaths.

Warrior II

- Switch sides (left leg forward).
- Hold for five breaths.

Downward Dog

- Hold for five breaths.
- Walk your feet toward your hands.
- Roll up to standing.
- Stand back in Mountain Pose.

Labeling Meditation

Find a comfortable seat where you can feel the balance of effort and ease in your body.

Set your timer for five minutes.

Close your eyes and bring your attention to your breath. Feel your inhale and feel your exhale.

You may notice that you quickly head off into thinking, planning, worrying, doubting. You may find that you feel tired or hungry.

Whatever you feel, when you realize it, notice it, label it, and go back to paying attention to your inhale and your exhale.

Action Step: Visualize

Read your goal to yourself. Pause and get still. Close your eyes and focus your attention on your goal. As clearly as you can, see yourself achieving that goal.

DAY ③

Mountain Pose

- Stand tall and roll your shoulders back.
- Press down through your feet and lengthen your spine.
- Gently press palm to palm at your heart.

Downward Dog

- Press your palms down.
- Bend your knees and walk your heels side to side to loosen up through your legs.
- Press your heels down toward the floor.
- Hold for five breaths.

Forward Lunge

- Bring your right foot forward into a lunge.
- Balance with your back heel off the floor and extend your hands over your head.
- Hold for five breaths.
- Switch legs and repeat.
- Hold for five breaths.

Downward Dog

- Hold for five breaths.

Warrior II

- Raise your right foot high and bring it forward into a lunge.
- Flatten your left foot on the floor behind you.
- Bend your right knee.
- Raise your arms up over your head and open wide to the sides.
- Focus your eyes on a point in front of you.
- Hold for five breaths.

Downward Dog

- Hold five breaths.

Warrior II

- Switch sides (left leg forward).
- Hold for five breaths.

Downward Dog

- Hold five breaths.
- Walk your feet toward your hands.
- Roll up to standing.

Airplane Pose into Warrior III

- Start in Mountain Pose.
- Focus on one point.
- Lift your right foot behind you and balance with your arms behind you, palms facing down.
- Keep your chest lifting and your spine long.
- Hold for three breaths. Then bring your arms out in front of you. Balance. Hold for two breaths.
- Switch sides and repeat.

Labeling Meditation

Find a comfortable seat where you can feel the balance of effort and ease in your body.

Set your timer for seven minutes.

Close your eyes and bring your attention to your breath. Feel your inhale and feel your exhale.

You may notice that you quickly head off into thinking, planning, worrying, doubting. You may find that you feel tired or hungry.

Whatever you feel, when you realize it, notice it, label it, and go back to paying attention to your inhale and your exhale.

Choose someone who can help you with some aspect of your goal.

Make a commitment to ask that person for help.

Write down your plan: I will ask _____ for/to _____ .

Do it!

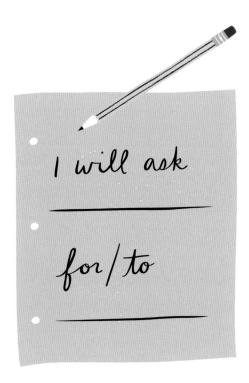

DAY ④

Mountain Pose

- Stand tall and roll your shoulders back.
- Press down through your feet and lengthen your spine.
- Gently press palm to palm at your heart.

Downward Dog

- Press your palms down.
- Bend your knees and walk your heels side to side to loosen up through your legs.
- Press your heels down toward the floor.
- Hold for five breaths.

Forward Lunge

- Bring your right foot forward into a lunge.
- Balance with your back heel off the floor and extend your hands over your head.
- Hold for five breaths.
- Switch legs and repeat.
- Hold for five breaths.

Downward Dog

• Hold for five breaths.

Warrior II

• Raise your right foot high and bring it forward into a lunge.

• Flatten your left foot on the floor behind you.

• Bend your right knee.

• Raise your arms up over your
head and open wide to the sides.

• Focus your eyes on a point in front of you.

• Hold for five breaths.

Downward Dog

• Hold five breaths.

Warrior II

• Switch sides (left leg forward).

• Hold for five breaths.

Downward Dog

• Hold five breaths.

• Walk your feet toward your hands.

• Roll up to standing.

Airplane Pose into Warrior III

- Start in Mountain Pose.
- Focus on one point.
- Lift your right foot behind you and
  balance with your arms behind
  you, palms facing down.
- Keep your chest lifting and your spine long.
- Hold for three breaths. Then bring your arms
  out in front of you. Balance. Hold for two breaths.
- Switch sides and repeat.

Tree Pose

- Lengthen through your spine.
- Rest your left foot on your right ankle
  or above the knee.
- Focus on one point and find your balance.
- Lift your arms out to the sides and then
  up over your head.
- Hold for five breaths.
- Switch sides and repeat.

 **Labeling Meditation**

Find a comfortable seat where you can feel the balance of effort and ease in your body.

Set your timer for ten minutes.

Close your eyes and bring your attention to your breath. Feel your inhale and feel your exhale.

You may notice that you quickly head off into thinking, planning, worrying, doubting. You may find that you feel tired or hungry.

Whatever you feel, when you realize it, notice it, label it, and go back to paying attention to your inhale and your exhale.

Remember: Patience is key. You may only notice one thought the whole time.

Action Step: Visualize

Read your goal to yourself. Pause and get still. Close your eyes and focus your attention on your goal. As clearly as you can, see yourself achieving that goal.

DAY ⑤

Mountain Pose

- Stand tall and roll your shoulders back.
- Press down through your feet and lengthen your spine.
- Gently press palm to palm at your heart.

Downward Dog

- Press your palms down.
- Bend your knees and walk your heels side to side to loosen up through your legs.
- Press your heels down toward the floor.
- Hold for five breaths.

Forward Lunge

- Bring your right foot forward into a lunge.
- Balance with your back heel off the floor and extend your hands over your head.
- Hold for five breaths.
- Switch legs and repeat.
- Hold for five breaths.

Downward Dog

- Hold for five breaths.

Warrior II

- Raise your right foot high and bring it forward into a lunge.
- Flatten your left foot on the floor behind you.
- Bend your right knee.
- Raise your arms up over your head and open wide to the sides.
- Focus your eyes on a point in front of you.
- Hold for five breaths.

Downward Dog

- Hold five breaths.

Warrior II

- Switch sides (left leg forward).
- Hold for five breaths.

Downward Dog

- Hold five breaths.
- Walk your feet toward your hands.
- Roll up to standing.

Airplane Pose into Warrior III

- Start in Mountain Pose.
- Focus on one point.
- Lift your right foot behind you and balance with your arms behind you, palms facing down.
- Keep your chest lifting and your spine long.
- Hold for three breaths. Then bring your arms out in front of you. Balance. Hold for two breaths.
- Switch sides and repeat.

Tree Pose

- Lengthen through your spine.
- Rest your left foot on your right ankle or above the knee.
- Focus on one point and find your balance.
- Lift your arms out to the sides and then up over your head.
- Hold for five breaths.
- Switch sides and repeat.

Horse Pose

- Stand with your feet spread out to the sides.
- Bend your knees.
- Press your palms together at your heart.
- Hold for five breaths.

Labeling Meditation

Find a comfortable seat where you can feel the balance of effort and ease in your body.

Set your timer for ten minutes.

Close your eyes and bring your attention to your breath. Feel your inhale and feel your exhale.

You may notice that you quickly head off into thinking, planning, worrying, doubting. You may find that you feel tired or hungry.

Whatever you feel, when you realize it, notice it, label it, and go back to paying attention to your inhale and your exhale.

Remember: Patience is key. You may only notice one thought the whole time.

Action Step: Take a Step Toward Your Goal

Start with a brainstorm: What are ten simple things that you could do to move toward your goal? Try to pick things you could reasonably do in the next twenty-four hours. If your goal is to "find a summer job," then that would not be on your list of ten steps to get there. You could instead put: "Call the Boys and Girls Club to find out where to get an application to be a camp counselor," for example.

Take out your journal or a piece of paper and number it one through ten. List ten things.

Even the smallest step brings you closer to success and

can improve your emotional and physical state. Resolve to take that first step:

Today I will _____.

1. _____
2. _____
3. _____
4. _____
5. _____
6. _____
7. _____
8. _____
9. _____
10. _____

Today I will

_____

Congratulations! You have completed
the **Personal Vision** Five-Day
Mindfulness Challenge!

You can't control the ocean,
but you can learn how to surf.
—JON KABAT–ZINN

GO WITH THE FLOW

DAY ①

Cat Tilt

- Inhale and look up, dropping your
  stomach toward the ground and curving your spine.
- Exhale and look toward your knees.
  Arch your spine.
- Repeat five times.

Thread the Needle

- On your hands and knees lift your right hand
  toward the sky and keep your focus on your right thumb.
- Bring your right forearm and elbow down
  behind your left arm.
- You can bring your shoulder all the way to the
  ground if that is comfortable.

Child Pose

- Press back and rest onto your heels.
- Bring your head to the floor with your
  arms out in front of you.
- Relax.
- Inhale and exhale (three times).

Ocean Breath Meditation

Sit with a balance of effort and ease.

Begin practicing this breath by imagining you have a mirror in front of you. Cup your hand and hold it near your mouth.

Inhale, and as you exhale, fog the mirror.

Try that two times.

Now imagine that there is a mirror in the back of your throat.

On your next inhale, fog the mirror at the back of your throat. (You will start to hear the beginning of the "ocean sound.")

Try that two times.

Next, try making the fogging breath with your mouth closed. It can seem a little odd at first, but after a bit you will be able to get the hang of it.

Inhale.

Exhale.

Set your timer for two minutes.

Close your eyes, and focus on your ocean breath.

Action Step: "Three Things" Exercise

This is a quick and easy way to practice taking a pause to be present.

Right now notice:

- Three Things You Can See (this can be anything: a window, your hand, a tree)
- Three Things You Can Hear (cars, birds, your own breath)
- Three Things You Can Feel (the chair, something in your pocket, your shirt on your back)

Use this exercise three times today. Pause and notice three things. . . .

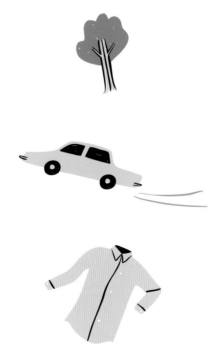

DAY ②

Cat Tilt

- Inhale and look up, dropping your stomach toward the ground and curving your spine.
- Exhale and look toward your knees.
- Arch your spine.
- Repeat five times.

Thread the Needle

- On your hands and knees lift your right hand toward the sky and keep your focus on your right thumb.
- Bring your right forearm and elbow down behind your left arm.
- You can bring your shoulder all the way to the ground if that is comfortable.
- Switch sides.

Child Pose

- Press back and rest onto your heels.
- Bring your head to the floor with your arms out in front of you.
- Relax.
- Inhale and exhale (three times).

Table Top (with one leg back)

- Come back onto your hands and knees.
- Inhaling, press your right leg straight out behind you. (Your palms stay planted on the ground.)
- Get long through your spine and hold your leg there.
- Hold for five breaths.
- Switch sides and extend your left leg straight out behind you.
- Hold for five breaths.

Mindfulness: Habit Change

Sometimes the best way to bring your attention to the moment is to change your habits. Try brushing your teeth using your opposite hand. Notice what feels unnatural and how much more aware you have to be to accomplish what is usually a fairly routine task.

Action Step: Observing Nature

You will need your journal or notebook for this exercise.

Go outside.

Find a comfortable place to sit, and plan to stay in this spot for ten minutes.

Look very closely at your surroundings.

Write down everything you see (the amount of clouds, the plants near you), everything you feel (the solidity of your seat, the temperature of the air), everything you hear, and everything you smell.

If you want to, sketch what you see as well.

Take your time. Look very closely at your surroundings.

Reflect:

I see _____.

I smell _____.

I hear _____.

I touch _____.

I feel _____.

I am thinking about _____.

I didn't expect _____.

DAY ③

Cat Tilt

- Inhale and look up, dropping your stomach toward the ground and curving your spine.
- Exhale and look toward your knees.
- Arch your spine.
- Repeat five times

Thread the Needle

- On your hands and knees lift your right hand toward the sky and keep your focus on your right thumb.
- Bring your right forearm and elbow down behind your left arm.
- You can bring your shoulder all the way to the ground if that is comfortable.
- Switch sides.

Child Pose

- Press back and rest onto your heels.
- Bring your head to the floor with your arms out in front of you.
- Relax.
- Inhale and exhale (three times).

Table Top (with one leg back)

- Come back onto your hands and knees.
- Inhaling, press your right leg straight out behind you. (Your palms stay planted on the ground.)
- Get long through your spine and hold your leg there.
- Hold for five breaths.
- Switch sides and extend your left leg straight out behind you.
- Hold for five breaths.

Side Angle

- Take your extended left foot and plant it on the ground.
- Keep your right knee bent on the ground.
- Shift your body to the side with your right hand pressing into the ground and your left hand reaching toward the sky. Your left leg is straight.
- Switch sides.

Mindfulness: Extending the Breath

Extending your inhale and exhale is a natural way to slow down and make sure you are giving your mind and body all of the oxygen needed. It is extremely relaxing.

Breathe normally for a moment as you prepare.

On your next breath, see if you can keep slowly inhaling for a count of four.

1 . . . 2 . . . 3 . . . 4.

On the exhale, follow that same, slow count.

1 . . . 2 . . . 3 . . . 4.

Repeat three more times.

Action Step: A Mindful Bite

Try this exercise during any meal.

Take two mindful bites, and see what you notice about:

• the color of the food

• the smell of the food

• the temperature

• the consistency

• each of the different flavors (spicy, salty, sweet)

• the speed and feel of your chewing

What else did you notice?

DAY

Cat Tilt

- Inhale and look up, dropping your
  stomach toward the ground and curving your spine.
- Exhale and look toward your knees.
  Arch your spine.
- Repeat five times.

Thread the Needle

- On your hands and knees, lift your
  right hand toward the sky and keep
  your focus on your right thumb.
- Bring your right forearm and elbow
  down behind your left arm.
- You can bring your shoulder all the
  way to the ground if that is comfortable.
- Switch sides.

Child Pose

- Press back and rest onto your heels.
- Bring your head to the floor with your
  arms out in front of you.
- Relax.
- Inhale and exhale (three times).

Table Top (with one leg back)

- Come back onto your hands and knees.
- Inhaling, press your right leg straight out behind you. (Your palms stay planted on the ground.)
- Get long through your spine and hold your leg there.
- Hold for five breaths.
- Switch sides and extend your left leg straight out behind you.
- Hold for five breaths.

Side Angle

- Take your extended left foot and plant it on the ground.
- Keep your right knee bent on the ground.
- Shift your body to the side with your right hand pressing into the ground and your left hand reaching toward the sky. Your left leg is straight.
- Switch sides.

Plank Pose to Side Plank

- Come into a plank pose,
  making as straight a line as possible with
  your body.
- Shift your weight into your left side
  and balance on your straight left arm
  and side of your left foot.
- Hold for three breaths.
- Move back into plank pose.
- Switch sides.
- Hold for three breaths.

Cobra Pose

- Release onto your stomach with the
  tops of your feet flat on the floor.
- Lift your head and chest, and bend
  your elbows, making sure they
  are directly under your shoulders.
- With your palms flat, gently press
  to help extend your spine.
- Hold for three breaths.
- Release.

For this exercise, choose an actual object—something you like to look at but that does not have any words on it.

Get into a comfortable seat and set the object where you can see it easily.

Set a timer for three minutes.

Keep your eyes gently open and look at your object.

Breathe normally and keep your attention on the object. Notice everything you can about it without actually picking it up.

You may find that even though your eyes are open, you forget what you are looking at from time to time as other thoughts take over.

That is fine. Just gently bring your attention back to your object.

Action Step: Creating without Judging
(a doodle exercise)

Sometimes it can be hard to create or try something new because you want everything to be perfect the first time you do it. That is human, but it is also not realistic or helpful. Here's an exercise to try to push through those habits of the mind that get in the way of your progress.

Get your journal or notebook, and quickly make a squiggle on the page—it can be anything.

Your job now is to turn it into something. Without paying attention to any negative mind chatter, just enjoy the feeling of the pen or pencil on the page and the playfulness of the task.

What did you create?

DAY ⑤

Cat Tilt

- Inhale and look up, dropping your stomach toward the ground and curving your spine.
- Exhale and look toward your knees. Arch your spine.
- Repeat five times.

Thread the Needle

- On your hands and knees, lift your right hand toward the sky and keep your focus on your right thumb.
- Bring your right forearm and elbow down behind your left arm.
- You can bring your shoulder all the way to the ground if that is comfortable.
- Switch sides.

Child Pose

- Press back and rest onto your heels.
- Bring your head to the floor with your arms out in front of you.
- Relax.
- Inhale and exhale (three times).

Table Top (with one leg back)

- Come back onto your hands and knees.
- Inhaling, press your right leg straight
  out behind you. (Your palms stay
  planted on the ground.)
- Get long through your
  spine and hold your leg there.
- Hold for five breaths.
- Switch sides and extend your left
  leg straight out behind you.
- Hold for five breaths.

Side Angle

- Take your extended left foot and plant
  it on the ground.
- Keep your right knee bent
  on the ground.
- Shift your body to the side
  with your right hand pressing into
  the ground and your left hand
  reaching toward the sky. Your left
  leg is straight.
- Switch sides.

Plank Pose to Side Plank

- Come into a plank pose, making as straight a line as possible with your body.
- Shift your weight into your left side and balance on your straight left arm and side of your left foot.
- Hold for three breaths.
- Move back into plank pose.
- Switch sides.
- Hold for three breaths.

Cobra Pose

- Release onto your stomach with the tops of your feet flat on the floor.
- Lift your head and chest, and bend your elbows, making sure they are directly under your shoulders.
- With your palms flat, gently press to help extend your spine.
- Hold for three breaths.
- Release.

Flying Squirrel Pose

- Rest on your stomach with the tops of your feet on the floor.
- Bring your hands to your sides.
- On an inhale, lift your arms and legs and chest off the floor.
- Leave your arms extended or try clasping them behind you if that is comfortable.
- Get long through your spine.
- Hold for three breaths.
- Release.
- Repeat two more times.

Super Human Pose

- Rest on your stomach with the tops of your feet flat on the floor.
- Bring your hands to the floor straight out in front of you.
- On an inhale, lift your arms and legs and chest off the floor with your hands reaching straight out in front.
- Get long through your spine.
- Hold for three breaths.
- Release.
- Repeat two more times.

Savasana

- Roll onto your back and rest in this relaxation pose for five to seven minutes.

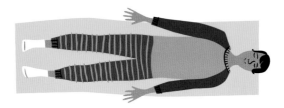

Mindfulness: Dandelion Breath

This breath is just like making a wish on a dandelion.

Cup your hand in front of your mouth.

Inhale through the nose.

Blow out through the mouth as if you could scatter all the dandelion seeds with one big gust.

Imagine that with this breath you are blowing away something that is making you tense.

Once or twice is great for releasing tension with the dandelion breath. If you feel light-headed, stop and breathe naturally.

Action Step: Walking Meditation

Take a ten-minute walk and use your senses to move through the following exercise.

First, notice how your body feels as you walk. Notice your feet hitting the ground, your legs, hips, and arms and how they are moving.

Notice your breath. How is it changing depending on your pace and the terrain? Pay attention.

Notice the air on your skin. Is it cool? Warm? Refreshing or clammy?

Now pay attention to what you can hear. Bring all of your awareness to the sounds around you. Notice whether they are natural or man-made.

Now focus on what you see. What is the light like, and is it different in different places? What colors stand out to you?

Congratulations! You have completed the Go With the Flow Five-Day Mindfulness Challenge!

BE YOURSELF.

Everyone else is taken.

—OSCAR WILDE

Be You

DAY ①

Seated Pose (with goal post arms)

- Sit with your legs crossed comfortably in front of you, your feet under your knees, and your back straight and tall.
- Hold your arms in "goal posts." Inhale and pull your arms back.
- Exhale and round your shoulders, bringing your arms forward—elbows toward each other (touching if you can).
- Repeat five times.

Arm Twist

- Bend your right elbow and pull it to your chest. Rest your right hand on the left shoulder.
- Hold for three breaths.
- Bend your left elbow and pull it to your chest. Rest your left hand on the right shoulder.
- Hold for three breaths.
- Repeat on both sides.

Finger Meditation

This is a quick and easy way to do a mini-meditation in the moment. Simply touch your thumb to each finger on your hand, saying silently:

Peace begins with me.

You can also replace the word *Peace* with anything that feels important to you:

Change begins with me.

Calm begins with me.

Or find another expression of it:

I am completely calm.

I am so strong.

I am confident here.

I am confident now.

Action Step: Color Your Word

Choose one word that expresses how you feel right now.

Take a piece of paper, and write down your word in big bubble or block letters in the center of the page.

Now choose your favorite colors to color it in.

Take your time. Pay attention to the shape of the paper, the smooth, flat surface, and pointy edges. Get so quiet that you can hear the sound of the pen or pencil on the page. How does it feels to move your hand across the page? What colors are you drawn to? Pay attention to what it feels like to push down and fill in the letters deeply, and what it feels like to just add a light brush of color. Vary it.

If you find yourself criticizing your work, just notice that and remind yourself that there is no right way to do this. Keep going.

DAY ②

Seated Pose (with goal post arms)

- Sit with your legs crossed comfortably in front of you, your feet under your knees, and your back straight and tall.
- Hold your arms in "goal posts." Inhale and pull your arms back.
- Exhale and round your shoulders, bringing your arms forward—elbows toward each other (touching if you can),
- Repeat five times.

Arm Twist

- Bend your right elbow and pull it to your chest. Rest your right hand on the left shoulder.
- Hold for three breaths.
- Bend your left elbow and pull it to your chest. Rest your left hand on the right shoulder.
- Hold for three breaths.
- Repeat on both sides.

Extended Arm Twist

- Bend your right elbow behind your head and place your left hand on the right elbow.
- Hold for three breaths.
- Bend your left elbow behind your head and place your right hand on the left elbow.
- Hold for three breaths.
- Repeat on both sides.

Seated Pose

- Sit with your legs crossed comfortably in front of you, your feet under your knees, and your back straight and tall.
- Bring your right foot into your hands.
- Press the sole of your foot with your thumbs.
- Hold your toes and rotate them back and forth.
- Interlace your fingers in between your toes and toggle and twist gently back and forth. (If that is too uncomfortable, just continue to hold and rotate the toes.)
- Circle your ankle in one direction and then the other.
- Switch sides.

Mindful "Wake Up" Breathing

This rejuvenating breathing exercise works in seconds to make you feel awake. It involves three quick inhalations through your nose and a long exhalation through your mouth. It is very effective. Start slow to get a sense of matching the breath and the movement, and then speed it up when you're ready.

Stand tall, with your feet hip-width apart, arms by your sides.

Let your knees gently bend.

For your first inhale, bring your arms straight out in front of you, parallel to the earth.

Then inhale again as you bring your hands out to the side.

Take your third inhale while swinging your arms up over your head.

Exhale and let your arms swing down as you bend your knees and fold forward with a long *haaaa* sound.

Try it again!

Action Step: Music Mindfulness

Choose a song or piece of music that you are familiar with, and see what it is like to focus on it completely. It could be your favorite song right now.

Play the song, and as you do, give it all of your attention. Listen as closely as you can, and try to hear something new.

- What instrument/s do you hear first?
- What other instruments do you hear? It doesn't matter if you know what they are called; just notice them as if you've never heard them before.
- Do you hear more than one singing voice?
- Pay attention to where the song changes.
  Where does it get faster, slower, louder, quieter?
- What do you feel when you listen to this song? Just notice your emotional and physical responses.
- What do you notice for the first time about this piece of music?

DAY ③

Seated Pose (with goal post arms)

- Sit with your legs crossed comfortably in front of you, your feet under your knees, and your back straight and tall.
- Hold your arms in "goal posts." Inhale and pull your arms back.
- Exhale and round your shoulders, bringing your arms forward—elbows toward each other (touching if you can).
- Repeat five times.

Arm Twist

- Bend your right elbow and pull it to your chest. Rest your right hand on the left shoulder.
- Hold for three breaths.
- Bend your left elbow and pull it to your chest. Rest your left hand on the right shoulder.
- Hold for three breaths.
- Repeat on both sides.

Extended Arm Twist

- Bend your right elbow behind your head and place your left hand on the right elbow.
- Hold for three breaths.
- Bend your left elbow behind your head and place your right hand on the left elbow.
- Hold for three breaths.
- Repeat on both sides.

Seated Pose

- Bring your right foot into your hands.
- Press the sole of your foot with your thumbs.
- Hold your toes and rotate them back and forth.
- Interlace your fingers in between your toes and toggle and twist gently back and forth. (If that is too uncomfortable, just continue to hold and rotate the toes.)
- Circle your ankle in one direction and then the other.
- Switch sides.

Lying on your back

- Hug your right knee into your chest.
- Position your right ankle across
  your left thigh (this is called Figure Four).
  Bring your arms around the left leg and
  gently pull toward your chest.
- Hold for five breaths.
- Switch legs.

Mindful Listening

For the next thirty seconds you are going to be still and focus on your sense of hearing.

(Set a timer if you'd like—otherwise, just know this will be brief.)

Sit comfortably. Place your hands in your lap or on your knees. You may try closing your eyes or looking down so you are less distracted by what you see and can focus everything on what you hear.

Begin:

Pay attention to everything you hear outside of the room (cars, the wind, birds, people).

What do you hear that you usually don't even notice?

Now what do you hear inside the room? Are there any

small noises you can hear when you are quiet? Can you hear anything in your own body? Your breathing? Your heartbeat?

Take a deep breath in and let a long breath out.

What did you notice?

How do you feel?

Action Step: Create Your Own Mindful Space

Create a visual reminder to pause in your day:

Try creating a peaceful spot in your room that will serve as a reminder to pause in your day. Maybe it is the top of your dresser, or a part of a shelf. When you look at it, it is your cue to notice how you are feeling now, in the present moment.

To create it, choose:

1. an item that has meaning to you
2. an item that makes you feel calm
3. an item from nature (which could be from outside or a photo or drawing)

This spot is now your visual reminder that all you need to do is pause, take a breath, and be here now.

DAY ④

Seated Pose (with goal post arms)

- Sit with your legs crossed comfortably in front of you, your feet under your knees, and your back straight and tall.
- Keep your arms in "goal posts." Inhale and pull your arms back.

- Exhale and round your shoulders, bringing your arms forward—elbows toward each other (touching if you can).
- Repeat five times.

Arm Twist

- Bend your right elbow and pull it to your chest. Rest your right hand on the left shoulder.
- Hold for three breaths.
- Bend your left elbow and pull it to your chest. Rest your left hand on the right shoulder.
- Hold for three breaths.
- Repeat on both sides.

Extended Arm Twist

- Bend your right elbow behind your head and place your left hand on the right elbow.
- Hold for three breaths.
- Bend your left elbow behind your head and place your right hand on the left elbow.
- Hold for three breaths.
- Repeat on both sides.

Seated Pose

- Bring your right foot into your hands.
- Press the sole of your foot with your thumbs.
- Hold your toes and rotate them back and forth.
- Interlace your fingers in between your toes and toggle and twist gently back and forth. (If that is too uncomfortable, just continue to hold and rotate the toes.)
- Circle your ankle in one direction and then the other.
- Switch sides.

Lying on your back

- Hug your right knee into your chest.
- Position your right ankle across your left thigh (this is called Figure Four). Bring your arms around the left leg and gently pull toward your chest.
- Hold for five breaths.
- Switch legs.

Extending with strap

You'll need a strap for this pose.

- Place the strap across the ball mound of your right foot.
- Extend the right leg (while keeping the left leg on the floor).
- Hold the strap in your right hand and open the right leg to the right.
- Hold and breathe.
  (See what is comfortable here.)
- Switch legs.

Counting Breath Meditation

Find a comfortable seat where you can feel the balance of effort and ease in your body.

Set your timer for five minutes.

Close your eyes and bring your attention to your breath.

Take a breath in and out and count 1.

Take a breath in and out and count 2.

Take a breath in and out and count 3.

Keep going until you reach 10. Most likely, you will lose track. That is fine; gently bring your attention back to the breath and start over. (The variation is to inhale 1 and exhale 2. Just do whichever feels more comfortable.)

Action Step: Affirmation

Create your own affirmation—a short statement that declares something positive about yourself:

I am happy.

I am smart.

I am great at singing.

I am a strong _____ (fill in the blank).

You don't have to find the perfect statement; just choose something that makes you feel good about yourself when you say it.

Say it out loud and take one deep breath in and out. Notice if you have any reaction to the statement. Whatever it is, just acknowledge it, but continue with the exercise.

Now see if you can remember to say it to yourself a minimum of five times over the next twenty-four hours. Maybe you will just remember it randomly or maybe it will be in response to some negative chatter that starts in your mind. Try to take that relaxing breath each time you remember it. At the end of the day, ask yourself, *How did it go? How did it make me feel?*

DAY ⑤

Seated Pose (with goal post arms)

- Sit with your legs crossed comfortably in front of you, your feet under your knees, and your back straight and tall.
- Keep your arms in "goal posts." Inhale and pull your arms back.
- Exhale and round your shoulders, bringing your arms forward. Elbows toward each other (touching if you can).
- Repeat five times.

Arm Twist

- Bend your right elbow and pull it to your chest. Rest your right hand on the left shoulder.
- Hold for three breaths.
- Bend your left elbow and pull it to your chest. Rest your left hand on the right shoulder.
- Hold for three breaths.
- Repeat on both sides.

Extended Arm Twist

- Bend your right elbow behind your head and place your left hand on the right elbow.
- Hold for three breaths.
- Bend your left elbow behind your head and place your right hand on the left elbow.
- Hold for three breaths.
- Repeat on both sides.

Seated Pose

- Bring your right foot into your hands.
- Press the sole of your foot with your thumbs.
- Hold your toes and rotate them back and forth.
- Interlace your fingers in between your toes and toggle and twist gently back and forth. (If that is too uncomfortable, just continue to hold and rotate the toes.)
- Circle your ankle in one direction and then the other.
- Switch sides.

Lying on your back

- Hug your right knee into your chest.
- Position your right ankle across your left thigh (this is called Figure Four). Bring your arms around the left leg and gently pull toward your chest.
- Hold for five breaths.
- Switch legs.

Extending with strap

You'll need a strap for this pose.

- Place the strap across the ball mound of your right foot.
- Extend the right leg (while keeping the left leg on the floor).
- Hold the strap in your right hand and open the right leg to the right.
- Hold and breathe. (See what is comfortable here.)
- Switch legs.

Extending with strap (across the body)

- Switch the strap into your left hand.
- Extend the right leg across your body to the left.
- Hold and breathe. (See what is comfortable here.)
- Straighten the right leg.

- Let go of the strap and bring the right leg to the floor slowly. (Allow twenty counts to get all the way down.)
- Notice the differences between the right and the left side.
- Switch sides and do the last three poses again.

Savasana

- End with five minutes of lying on your back in Savasana pose for total relaxation.

Counting Breath Meditation

Find a comfortable seat where you can feel the balance of effort and ease in your body.

Set your timer for five minutes to begin.

Close your eyes and bring your attention to your breath.

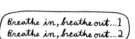

Breathe in, breathe out...1
Breathe in, breathe out...2

Take a breath in and out and count 1.

Take a breath in and out and count 2,

Take a breath in and out and count 3.

Keep going until you reach 10. Most likely, you will lose track. That is fine; gently bring your attention back to the breath and start over.

(The variation is to inhale 1 and exhale 2. Just do whichever feels more comfortable.).

Action Step: Affirmations

Choose the same affirmation from yesterday, or create a new one.

Say it out loud and take one deep breath in and out.

Now, see if you can remember to say it to yourself a minimum of five times over the next twenty-four hours. Maybe you will just remember it randomly or maybe it will be in response to some negative chatter that starts in your mind. Try to take that relaxing breath each time you remember it.

At the end of the day, ask yourself, *How did it go? How did it make me feel?*

Congratulations! You have completed
the **Be You** Five-Day Mindfulness Challenge!

NOTES

INTRODUCTION

1. Referencing: Monkey mind, p. 3

Alice G. Walton, "8 Science-Based Tricks for Quieting The Monkey Mind," *Forbes*, February 28, 2017, https://www.forbes.com/sites/alicegwalton/2017/02/28/8-science -based-tricks-for-quieting-the-monkey-mind/#1707ea4b1af6.

BJ Gallagher, "Buddha: How to Tame Your Monkey Mind," *The Huffington Post*, last updated November 3, 2011, http://www.huffingtonpost.com/bj-gallagher/buddha -how-to-tame-your-m_b_945793.html.

Sarah Rudell Beach, "Teaching Mindfulness to Teens: 5 Ways to Get 'Buy In,'" Left Brain Buddha: The Modern Life, accessed October 1, 2017, http://leftbrainbuddha.com/teaching-mindfulness-to-teens-5-ways-get-buy/.

"Monkey Mind, The," Guide to Buddhism A to Z, accessed January 15, 2017, http://www.buddhisma2z.com/content.php?id=274.

"Understanding the Monkey Mind & How to Live in Harmony with Your Mental Companion," Pocket Mindfulness, accessed October 15, 2017, https://www.pocketmindfulness.com/understanding-monkey-mind-live-harmony -mental-companion/.

CHAPTER ONE. MINDFULNESS

2. Referencing: Two Monks story, p. 10

Ahihalau. "Two Monks and a Woman—a Zen Lesson," Stories of Kindness from Around the World, Kind Spring, last updated June 20, 2014, http://www.kindspring.org/story/view.php?sid=63753.

Harriet Lerner, PhD, "An Unforgettable Zen Story About 'Letting Go,'" *Psychology Today*, updated March 8, 2015, https://www.psychologytoday.com/blog/the-dance-connection/201503/unforgettable -zen-story-about-letting-go.

3. Referencing: Pac-Man reference to cells/immune system functioning, p. 13

Rick Harrington, *Stress, Health and Well-Being: Thriving in the 21st Century* (California: Wadsworth Publishing, 2013), 110–113.

Ken Kingery, "Regenerating Damaged Nerves with 'Pac-Man' Cells," Duke University

Biomedical Engineering, June 12, 2017, https://bme.duke.edu/about/news /regenerating-damaged-nerves-pac-man-cells.

4. Referencing: Mindfulness resulting in less social and academic stress, p. 14
Srividya Ramasubramanian, "Mindfulness, Stress Coping and Everyday Resilience Among Emerging Youth in a University Setting: A Mixed Method Approach," http://www.tandfonline.com/doi/full/10.1080/02673843.2016.1175361?scroll= top&needAccess=true.

"Just Breathe: Mindfulness May Help Freshman Stress Less and Smile More," Science Daily, April 20, 2017, https://www.sciencedaily.com/releases /2017/04/170420090204.htm.

5. Referencing: Farmer story, p. 20
Richard Smith, PhD, "It Takes Patience to Know Bad Luck From Good Luck," *Psychology Today*, March 19, 2015, https://www.psychologytoday.com/blog/joy-and -pain/201503/it-takes-patience-know-bad-luck-good-luck.

Judy Simon, "We'll See—A Zen Story," BuddhistInspiration, December 20, 2011, http://buddhistinspiration.blogspot.com/2011/12/well-see-zen-story.html.

CHAPTER THREE. MINDFUL BREATHING
6. Referencing: Dr. Benson's work, p. 87.
Herbert Benson, MD, with Miriam Klipper, *The Relaxation Response* (New York: William Morrow, 1975), xviii–xxiv, 126–132.

Marilyn Mitchell, MD, "Dr. Herbert Benson's Relaxation Response," *Psychology Today*, March 29, 2013, https://www.psychologytoday.com/blog/heart-and-soul -healing/201303/dr-herbert-benson-s-relaxation-response.

CHAPTER FOUR. MINDFUL MEDITATION
7. Referencing: Harvard studies, p. 105
Sue McGreevey, "Meditations' Positive Residual Effects," *Harvard Gazette*, November 13, 2012, https://news.harvard.edu/gazette/story/2012/11/meditations -positive-residual-effects/.

Sue McGreevey, "Turn Down the Volume," *Harvard Gazette*, April 22, 2011, https://news.harvard.edu/gazette/story/2011/04/turn-down-the-volume/.

8. Referencing: Thought Trains, p. 105

Dzung X. Vo, MD, *The Mindful Teen: Powerful Skills to Help You Handle Stress One Moment at a Time* (Oakland, California: Instant Help: 2015), 114–116.

Note: He is also referencing this workbook: Gina M. Biegel, *The Stress Reduction Workbook for Teens: Mindfulness Skills to Help You Deal with Stress* (Oakland, California: New Harbinger Publications, 2010).

"Meditation Mondays: Train Station," Living Dharma Now: Thoughts on Living a Buddhist Lifestyle, April, 2011, https://livingdharmanow.wordpress.com/2011/04/26/meditation-mondays-train-station/.

9. Reference: Meditation supports the brain's functioning, p. 111

Peter Kelley, "Mindful Multitasking: Meditation First Can Calm Stress, Aid Concentration," University of Washington News, June 13, 2012, http://www.washington.edu/news/2012/06/13/mindful-multitasking-meditation-first-can-calm-stress-aid-concentration/.

RJ Davidson, J Kabat-Zinn, J Schumacher, M Rosenkranz, D Muller, SF Santorelli, F Urbanowski, A Harrington, K Bonus, JF Sheridan, "Alterations in Brain and Immune Function Produced by Mindfulness Meditation," *Psychosomatic Medicine*, July 2003, https://www.ncbi.nlm.nih.gov/pubmed/12883106.

10. Reference: Effects of kindness meditation, p. 119

BE Kok, KA Coffey, MA Cohn, LI Catalino, T Vacharkulksemsuk, SB Algoe, M Brantley, BL Fredrickson, "How Positive Emotions Build Physical Health: Perceived Positive Social Connections Account for the Upward Spiral Between Positive Emotions and Vagal Tone," *Psychology Science*, July 1, 2013, https://www.ncbi.nlm.nih.gov/pubmed/23649562.

David Desteno, "The Kindness Cure," *The Atlantic*, July 21, 2015, https://www.the-atlantic.com/health/archive/2015/07/mindfulness-meditation-empathy-compassion/398867/.

11. Reference: Peace begins with me, p. 121

Gabrielle Bernstein, "Mantra Meditation (Based on the Teaching of Yogi Bhajan)," Lululemon, November 13, 2015, https://www.youtube.com/watch?v=eiLWO9jOTao.

BIBLIOGRAPHY

Bhanoo, Sindya N. "How Meditation May Change the Brain." *The New York Times*, January 28, 2011. https://well.blogs.nytimes.com/2011/01/28/how-meditation-may -change-the-brain/.

Boorstein, Sylvia. *It's Easier Than You Think: The Buddhist Way to Happiness*. New York: HarperCollins, 1995.

Farhi, Donna. *The Breathing Book: Good Health and Vitality Through Essential Breath Work*. New York: Holt Paperbacks, 1996.

Gates, Rolf, and Katrina Kenison. *Meditations from the Mat: Daily Reflections on the Path of Yoga*. New York: Anchor Books, 2002.

Goleman, Daniel, and Richard J. Davidson. *Altered Traits: Science Reveals How Meditation Changes Your Mind, Brain, and Body*. New York: Avery/Penguin, 2017.

Hölzel, BK, J Carmody, KC Evans, EA Hoge, JA Dusek, L Morgan, RK Pitman, and SW Lazar. "Stress Reduction Correlates with Structural Changes in the Amygdala." Social Cognition Affect Neuroscience, March, 2010. https://www.ncbi.nlm.nih.gov /pubmed/19776221.

Jones, Rachel. "Learning to Pay Attention." PLOS Biology, May 8, 2007. http://journals.plos.org/plosbiology/article?id=10.1371/journal.pbio.0050166.

Lutz, Antoine, Julie Brefczynski-Lewis, Tom Johnstone, and Richard J. Davidson. "Regulation of the Neural Circuitry of Emotion by Compassion Meditation: Effects of Meditative Expertise." PLOS ONE (March 26, 2008). http://journals.plos.org /plosone/article?id=10.1371/journal.pone.0001897.

Kabat-Zinn, Jon. *Mindfulness for Beginners: Reclaiming the Present Moment and Your Life*. Colorado: Sounds True, 2012.

Kaufman, Keith. "New Mindfulness Methods Helps Coaches, Athletes Score," American Psychological Association, August 4, 2017. https://www.sciencedaily.com/releases/2017/08/170804091350.htm.

Kerr, Catherine , Matthew D. Sacchet, Sara W. Lazar, Christopher I. Moore, and Stephanie R. Jones. "Mindfulness starts with the body: somatosensory attention and top-down modulation of cortical alpha rhythms in mindfulness meditation." Frontiers in Human Neuroscience, February 13, 2013. http://journal.frontiersin.org /article/10.3389/fnhum.2013.00012/full.

McGreevey, Sue. "Eight Weeks to a Better Brain." *Harvard Gazette*, January 21, 2011. https://www.sciencedaily.com/releases/2011/01/110121144007.htm.

Pocket Mindfulness. "Understanding the Monkey Mind & How to Live in Harmony with Your Mental Companion." Accessed October 15, 2017. https://www.pocketmindfulness.com/understanding-monkey-mind-live-harmony -mental-companion/.

Rios, Mauricio Murga. "Brief Mindfulness Training May Boost Test Scores, Working Memory." Association for Psychology Science, March 26, 2013. http://www.psychologicalscience.org/news/releases/brief-mindfulness-training-may -boost-test-scores-working-memory.html.

Siegel, Dan. "Mindfulness and Neural Integration." Posted May 2, 2012 at TEDxStudioCityED, Video, 18:26.

Siegel, Daniel J. *Brainstorm: The Power and Purpose of the Teenage Brain*. New York: Tarcher/Penguin, 2013.

Sweet, Corinne. *The Mindfulness Journal: Exercises to Help You Find Peace and Calm Wherever You Are*. London: Boxtree/Pan Macmillan, 2016.

Vranich, Belisa, Dr. *Breathe: The Simple, Revolutionary 14-Day Program to Improve Your Mental and Physical Health*. New York: St. Martin's Griffin, 2016.

Watts, Alan, and Al Chung-liang Huang, *TAO: The Watercourse Way*. New York: Pantheon/Penguin, 1975.

Williams, Mark, and Danny Penman. *Mindfulness: An Eight-Week Plan for Finding Peace in a Frantic World*. New York: Rodale, 2011.

RESOURCES

BOOKS

Bernstein, Gabrielle. *The Universe Has Your Back: Transform Fear to Faith*. California: Hay House Inc., 2016.

Brower, Elena. *Practice You: A Journal*. Colorado: Sounds True, 2017.

Budig, Kathryn. *The Women's Health Big Book of Yoga*. New York: Rodale Books, 2012.

Collard, Patricia. *The Little Book of Mindfulness: 10 Minutes a Day to Less Stress, More Peace*. London: Gaia Books, 2014.

Farrarons, Emma. *The Mindfulness Coloring Book: Anti-Stress Art Therapy for Busy People*. New York: The Experiment Publishing, 2015.

Harper, Jennifer Cohen. *Yoga & Mindfulness Practices for Teens Card Deck*. Wisconsin: PESI Publishing, 2017.

Kabat-Zinn, Jon. *Wherever You Go, There You Are: Mindfulness Meditation in Everyday Life*. New York: Hachette Books, 2005.

Martin, Cory. *Yoga for Beginners: Simple Yoga Poses to Calm Your Mind and Strengthen Your Body*. California: Rockridge Press, 2015.

Nan, Thich Nhat, and Vo-Dihn Mai. *The Miracle of Mindfulness: An Introduction to the Practice of Meditation*. Boston: Beacon Press, 1999.

Patel, Meera Lee. *Start Where You Are: A Journal for Self-Exploration*. New York: Perigee, 2015.

Salgado, Brenda. *Real World Mindfulness for Beginners: Navigate Daily Life One Practice at a Time*. California: Sonoma Press, 2016.

Saltzman, Amy, MD. *A Still Quiet Place: A Mindfulness Program for Teaching Children and Adolescents to Ease Stress and Difficult Emotions*. California: New Harbinger Publications, 2014.

Tarkeshi, Jasmine. *Yoga Body and Mind Handbook: Easy Poses, Guided Meditations, Perfect Peace Wherever You Are*. California: Sonoma Press, 2017.

Vo, Dzung X., MD. *The Mindful Teen: Powerful Skills to Help You Handle Stress One Moment at a Time*. Oakland, California: Instant Help, 2015.

ONLINE GUIDANCE AND CLASSES

Curvy Yoga Studio
https://www.curvyyoga.com/

Gaia
https://www.gaia.com/yoga/practices

YogaGlo
https://www.yogaglo.com/

Yoga Today
https://www.yogatoday.com/

YogaVibes
https://www.yogavibes.com/

APPS

Headspace
https://www.headspace.com/headspace-meditation-app

Insight Timer
https://insighttimer.com/

Pocket Yoga
http://www.pocketyoga.com/

Smiling Mind
https://www.smilingmind.com.au/smiling-mind-app/

Stop, Breathe & Think
https://www.stopbreathethink.com/

10% Happier
http://www.10percenthappier.com/mindfulness-meditation-the-basics/

Yoga Studio
http://www.yogastudioapp.com

Acknowledgments

There are so many people I want to thank at this point, as it takes a village to write a book or do absolutely anything that matters in life. I am so grateful to Lauri Hornik, and the team at Dial Books, for their focus and clarity and for wanting to create books that inspire. A heartfelt thanks to my agent, Faye Bender, for her enthusiasm every step of the way. To Libby VanderPloeg, you are a genius. To Leigh Standley for always reminding me that "fortune favors . . ." Leslie, Bruce, Brenna, et al, thank you for your honesty and for being part of my team. I am grateful to Brian Leaf for his wise counsel and to Adrian Zackheim and Kate Cortesi for being in my corner. To Ben, Bekah, Sarah, and Alex, how did I get so lucky? To Rolf Gates, thank you for being my friend and partner in all things and for making every single day an adventure. And to Jasmine and Dylan, you two are everything and you make me want to make this world a better place.